How to Make Homilies Better, Briefer, *and* **Bolder**

Tips from a Master Homilist

How to Make Homilies Better, Briefer, *and* Bolder

Tips from a Master Homilist

Alfred McBride, O.Praem.

Preface by Archbishop Timothy M. Dolan

Our Sunday Visitor Publishing Division
Our Sunday Visitor, Inc.
Huntington, IN 46750

Table of Contents

—∞∞∞—

Preface

Pardon the cliché — the author does not want to use them while preaching — but this book is "just what the doctor ordered."

We bishops, priests, and deacons have as our primary task (*Presbyterorum*, 4) to preach the Gospel. In the '50s, we were told a good sermon should be a catechism lesson on a doctrinal and moral teaching; in the '60s, we heard that a good sermon — pardon me, a homily — should be an exegesis of the biblical readings of the liturgy of the Word; in the '70s, we were instructed that we needed to share feelings and bring in psychology; in the '80s, we were mandated to "tell stories." By the '90s, we did not know *what* to do.

What we did know is that our people were not happy with our preaching. As hard as we had tried, study after study told us the bad news that our folks were upset with our homilies. Some even blamed our poor pulpit skills for the severe drop in Mass attendance, as we watched many of our people exit for churches offering more dazzling, provocative, and better prepared preaching.

So I have yet to meet a brother bishop, priest, or deacon who is not searching for help in his preaching.

Start with Fr. Alfred McBride's book. It is simple, succinct, short — come to think of it, all necessary elements of an effective homily!

He himself has been preaching for fifty-three years, at Mass, on retreats, at conferences. He has also taught the course called "homiletics" to future priests and deacons. To listen to him preach is a joy, as he speaks from the soul, heeds God's Word, teaches sound doctrine, exhorts to virtue, all in a sincere, captivating manner. He writes the same way.

A wonderful strategy in this work is that we visit the "classroom of the ages" as Fr. McBride "practices what he preaches," concretizing the practical points with lessons from the towering preachers of the past, drinking of the wisdom and sanctity of women and men from our Catholic tradition, as pertinent today as they were centuries ago.

My own study of Church history has led me to conclude that every period of genuine renewal in the Church has been characterized by a revival of sound preaching. Pope John Paul II and Pope Benedict XVI have both observed that we are indeed on the brink of such a period of renewal, a "Springtime of evangelization." *Ergo* . . . it's shock-paddle time for our preaching!

Start here . . . you'll appreciate it. So will your people.

— TIMOTHY M. DOLAN
Archbishop of Milwaukee
Holy Thursday, 2007

Introduction

⸻⸺⸻

It is the first task of priests . . . to preach the Gospel of God to all.

— *PRESBYTERORUM ORDINIS*, 4

Among other tasks, it is the task of deacons to assist the bishops and priests . . . in the proclamation of the Gospel and preaching.

— *CATECHISM OF THE CATHOLIC CHURCH*, 1570

Gather your people to the word of doctrine like a nurse who cherishes her children.

— ORDINATION RITE OF ALEXANDRIAN CHURCH

The Acts of the Apostles tells us that the first ministerial act in the history of the Church was preaching the Gospel. Throughout all of our history, preaching is a constant. The liturgy of the Word, in one way or another, has accompanied the liturgy of the Eucharist. People need to be called to faith in order to believe. They need nourishment to grow in the faith they profess. "Faith comes from what is heard, and what is heard comes from the word of Christ" (Rom. 10:17).

From the time of my ordination in 1953, and throughout my priesthood, I have always had an interest in preaching better, briefer, and bolder. I was helped in this quest by the privilege of teaching homiletics for five years at St. Norbert Abbey and, again, for nine years at Blessed John Seminary in Weston, Massachusetts. I learned a great deal from my students as well as from listening to popes, bishops, priests, and deacons preaching in a variety of settings. As you will see from this book, I found a large number of helpful hints from books on public speaking and preaching.

When I started to write the book, I felt the need to draw some lessons from Church history's greatest preachers, both those who are canonized saints and more recent men and women who were outstanding speakers and holy witnesses to Christ. Generally, I looked for a trait from their life stories that can help us in our homilies, such as the personal intimacy accomplished by Augustine, the defense of the Incarnation from Leo the Great, the love of the Bible shown by Jerome, and Chrysostom's passion for Christian morality.

You will note that I include several women as well. I know they do not give homilies, but they illustrate qualities and talents that benefit preachers. Catherine of Siena shows us how to speak truth to power, as she did for Pope Gregory XI. Thérèse of Lisieux is my pick to help us with children's homilies by means of her way of spiritual childhood. Thea Bowman was an ardent preacher and public speaker who opened us to the needs of Catholic African Americans, especially in the field of education.

I am grateful to the Society for the Propagation of the Faith for their permission to reprint one of Archbishop Fulton Sheen's most memorable TV presentations, "How to Talk." I remember the night he gave it, and I retained many of his lessons over the years. Sheen was a master preacher who excelled beyond all his contemporaries and convinced us that "Life Is Worth Living."

Along with all these opening stories, I offer practical advice in a number of areas: how to overcome fear of preaching; tips for wedding, funeral, and children's homilies; themes for preaching during the major liturgical seasons; and sources I have found helpful. I emphasize several basics of preaching:

- Link your homily to the liturgy of the day.
- Make your homily relevant to your listeners.
- Make only one point.
- Start with a story.
- Know how you are going to end.

Don't read your homily. Try to preach without notes. Keep eye contact with your congregation. Use lots of examples. Say the teaching and give it a word picture. Share with your people what your life experience has taught you, but don't concentrate on yourself. Make your homily a prayer and not a performance. Use humor wisely. Don't look for praise. Give God the glory.

Let me close with a story from the life of Mister Rogers, who, I was surprised to learn, was a trained Presbyterian minister.

Toward the end of his seminary days, he used to attend services at different churches to experience a variety of preaching approaches. On one occasion, he went with a friend to a church whose pastor was an exceptionally good preacher. Fred Rogers was disappointed to find out that a supply preacher — "elderly at that," he said — was the minister for the service instead.

The man was uninspiring. Fred spent the time mentally checking all the ways in which the preacher was bending, breaking, or ignoring every homiletic rule. At its conclusion, he turned to his friend to share his frustrations — only to see tears flowing down her cheeks. "He said everything I needed to hear," she told him.

How could such a poor sermon have touched her? He then realized what caused the differing reactions. She had come with a need. He arrived as a judge. Her need met the sincerity of the old preacher and made it possible for the Holy Spirit to translate an awkward sermon into a message the woman needed to hear. (Adapted from *The Simple Faith of Mister Rogers*, by Amy Hollingsworth, Integrity Press, Nashville, 2005, pp. 33-34.)

The space between the lectern and the people is holy ground, the space where the Spirit not only translates our weak words and clumsy thoughts but transcends our humble offerings to make them God's words for the joy and healing of the hearts of your listeners. What you offer your people in faith can be translated by the Holy Spirit to meet their many needs.

I am very thankful for the honor of having Archbishop Timothy M. Dolan present the preface to this book. He has a joyful heart and a love of preaching that regularly touches his vast congregation.

— REV. ALFRED MCBRIDE, O.PRAEM.
St. Norbert Abbey, De Pere, Wisconsin

ONE

Let God's Word Own You

The secret of St. Augustine's preaching...
from Peter Brown's Augustine of Hippo

Augustine would not have been physically isolated from his audience. The congregation of Hippo stood throughout the sermon, while Augustine usually sat back on his *cathedra*. The first row, therefore, would have met their bishop roughly at eye level, only some five yards distance....

The scriptural idea of "breaking bread," of "feeding the multitude," by expounding the Bible, an idea already rich with complex associations, is central to Augustine's view of himself as a preacher. "I go to feed so that I can give you to eat. I am the servant, the bringer of food, not the master of the house. I lay out before you that from which I also draw my life." As he told Jerome, he could never be a disinterested Biblical scholar. "If I do gain any knowledge of the scriptures, I pay it out immediately to the people of God...."

Augustine was able to communicate to a congregation his contemplative ascent to God. He could reduce the inhabitants of a whole town to tears, but he would have owed his position as a "star" preacher to the quite characteristic way in which he would settle back in his chair, and like the inspired teacher he had always been, get his listeners to identify themselves with his own excitement at unraveling a difficult text.

"Let me try to winkle out the hidden secrets of this Psalm we have just sung, and chip a sermon out of it to satisfy your ears and minds. I confess this is a problem. *Knock and it shall be opened unto you*: knock by concentrating hard; knock by showing a keen interest; knock even for me, that I should extract something from it that is worthwhile telling you."

— PETER BROWN, *AUGUSTINE OF HIPPO*,
UNIVERSITY OF CALIFORNIA PRESS, BERKELEY, 1975, PP. 251–4

If you never had the joy of reading Peter Brown's remarkable study of Augustine, take the time to do it soon. For Augustine's approach to preaching, read Brown's chapters *Populus Dei* (from which the preceding quote comes) and *Doctrina Christiana*.

Stay in Touch with Your Listeners

What have I learned from what I just cited?

Don't be isolated from your listeners. Think of your relationship with them as a communion. Be up close and personal. Let people see your eyes. They are the windows of your soul, of the conviction you bring to your interpretation of God's Word. If you need them, take your notes with you, but don't let them get in the way of being in touch with your congregation. Many of the suggestions I offer you in this book are ways to create union with your people. Your delivery, your capacity to put people at ease, your very desire to communicate, brings you closer to your listeners.

I was at St. Patrick's Cathedral in New York City a number of times when Cardinal John O'Connor was celebrant and homilist. He loved preaching and liked getting near his people in that cavernous church. He would stand on the top step of the sanctuary, right in the middle, with a few notes in his hand, a mind full of ideas, and a heart full of prayer. He projected well and was very effective. When Mayor Koch (who was Jewish) was in the first pew, O'Connor would say to him, "How'm I doing?" Koch would always laugh, smile, and nod — immediate positive feedback!

I have watched homilists preach with downcast eyes, as though they are having a private conversation with themselves. I have seen others who firmly look at the back wall of the church. But people know when a speaker is ignoring them, and today's congregations want the homilist to look at them. Find a friendly face and take courage from that to see with whom you wish to communicate.

Just as Augustine shared his contemplative ascent to God, bring your relationship to God to your homily. For that, of course, you must have a life of prayer. Your homily needs to be soaked with prayer and convey that you are someone near to God. This is not spiritual bragging or unseemly preoccupation with your self-concerns. This is a matter of people's need to sense that you are not just talking *about* God but come to them bearing God's very presence.

Break bread, so you can feed the multitude. "Breaking the bread" of Scripture means approaching it as the living Word of God. Never make your homily a dry interlude of scholarly data about the text. By all means, study the fruits of scholarship to be sure your interpretation is sound, but make that the servant of your homily, not its master. Learn to dialogue with the Word — an act that includes speaking from your heart and listening with your soul.

Imitate the Prophets

Imitate the preaching style of the prophets. Notice how conscious they are of divine revelation: *The word of the Lord came to me.* Each day you pick up the Lectionary, you have the opportunity to say those same words. The Church makes it possible for the word of the Lord to come to you. Page after page of Scripture is an avalanche of God's almost impetuous outpouring of what he wants us to know about his loving plan to save us, and even about the intimate life of the divine.

Prophets feel so close to God that when they preach they feel they are *nabiim* (mouthpieces), humble servants of the divine words. We are called to relay God's own words both directly and in a contemporary idiom and relevant application. Our faith is a revelation-based religion. The Fathers of the Church never tire of feeding themselves with Scripture and paying it out to their spiritually hungry listeners.

Hearing Is Believing

Concentrate on the fact that Scripture is directed to the ear, not the eye. *Hear the word of the Lord.* The visual culture of TV and the Internet may convince you that "seeing is believing," but the Church trusts in the interior power of the spoken word of God for the nurturing of people's faith.

> But how are men to call on him in whom they have not believed?
> And how are they to believe in him of whom they have never heard?
> And how are they to hear without a preacher? And how can men

preach unless they are sent? . . . So faith comes from what is heard, and what is heard comes by the preaching of Christ.

— Rom. 10:14–15, 17

GUIDES TO PREACHING THE LITURGICAL SCRIPTURE READINGS

1. Search for a theme that unites the readings. This can often be done between the first reading and the Gospel.
2. Suggestion: once a month, preach on the *second* reading.
3. At beginning of the liturgical year, take time to get an overview of the readings, especially the Gospels. Look for themes that unite blocks of readings — say, in six-week sections. This eliminates the disparate and choppy feeling listeners get when a homilist treats each Sunday Gospel in isolation.
4. Never forget that the homily on Scripture is a proclamation of divine revelation. The homilist is like a prophet — a mouthpiece of God — relaying God's own words in a contemporary idiom and application.
5. Call the listeners to faith, to a "Yes" to God's revelatory invitation. Every homily is a dialogue of salvation, a dynamic of divine revelation and a human faith response — an "Amen, Lord!"
6. Apply the message of God's Word to the doctrinal, spiritual, and moral lives of the listeners. This is the *So what?* of the message. A homily is not a lecture; it is motivation, urging, and invitation — a "Let us march."
7. Avoid making the homily a dry interlude of scholarly data about the text. The homilist should know the fruits of Scripture scholarship so that his interpretation is sound, but he needs to use it to bring the magnificent Words of God alive, sumptuous, and vibrant with the faith experience that accompanied the original revelation.

Do not lose confidence in the power of the spoken word, especially one that illumines the word of God. While St. Francis says, "Preach always. Sometimes, use words," the homilist is obliged to preach a *lot* and use *many* words. Pope Paul VI connects the dots when he says that people today do not listen to teachers; they listen to witnesses. So, because his teachers (and preachers) are, first of all, witnesses, the effective homilist is also a witness to what he preaches. He preaches what he practices. That makes it easier for him to be confident in the power of the spoken word and the durability of the adage "Hearing is believing."

The "So What" of the Homily

One of the reasons the homilies of the Fathers of the Church still have relevance today is that the homilists were pastors in touch with the needs of their people, not simply scholars in ivory towers. Even Jerome, who was less obviously a pastor, often delivered his talks with an eye on the behavioral needs of his audience. Most of the others — like Ambrose, Chrysostom, and Augustine — were busy bishops whose lively homilies echoed with the pastoral needs of their people.

This is what we lightly refer to as the "so what" of our homilies. A homily is more than an abstract "think piece" about the Bible. When Benedict XVI preached to a group of children about frequent confession, he used the illustration of the need to clean house regularly. It's the same house, with much the same dust, grime, and other cleaning needs. It has to be kept up or it will deteriorate. So it is with our souls. They need "house-cleaning." This homey application gets the point across and is all the more admirable coming from a distinguished theologian who is now a universal pastor.

Generally, most active parish priests are aware of this need and are more than expert on practical applications. With the challenges from increasing secularization in our culture, it would appear that our people need more guidance on how to remain active Christians in these circumstances. Let God's Word own you. Stay in touch with your congregation. Break the bread of Scripture to feed the crowd. Preach like a prophet. Recall that "hearing is believing." Apply God's Word to the doctrinal, spiritual, and moral lives of the people in real-life, concrete ways.

How effective am I in giving Scripture-based homilies?

O God, do not help me to preach better. Help me to *be* better.

— Calvin Miller

Homilies do not have to be eternal to be immortal.

— Robert Cook

TWO

Call People to Faith

The preacher: St. John Chrysostom (347–407)

Preaching makes me healthy. As soon as I open my mouth all tiredness is gone.

— JOHN CHRYSOSTOM, HOMILY COMMENT

As a teen in Antioch, John Chrysostom was "ensnared by the lusts of the world," even as he was receiving a classical education. After a religious conversion at eighteen, he was tutored for three years in Scripture by Diodorus. After that, he joined some monks for three years on a nearby mountain to grow in prayer and spirituality. He completed his spiritual training by living as a hermit for two more years. Then, upon his return to Antioch, Bishop Flavian of Antioch ordained him a deacon, during which time he demonstrated his developing preaching gift that one day would earn him the title Chrysostom, the "golden mouth." As a priest, he delivered hundreds of homilies on Scripture and moral issues. Listened to with enthusiasm and recorded by secretaries, these works earned him the title Father of the Church.

Chrysostom was always improving his preaching, ever raising the bar. What he said of St. Paul's quest for excellence as a preacher and courageous defender of the faith was true of himself:

> Each day Paul aimed ever higher; each day he rose up with greater ardor and faced with new eagerness the dangers that threatened him. . . . He was far more eager for the shameful abuse that his zeal in preaching brought upon him than we are for the most pleasing honors. . . . The most important thing of all to him was that he knew he was loved by Christ.
>
> — LITURGY OF THE HOURS, VOL. III, P. 1322

Like St. Paul, John Chrysostom understood that his greatest homily always lay ahead of him.

MAKE ONE POINT

When it comes to preaching, a rifle is better than buckshot. Look at a dog gnawing a bone and notice the concentration and sense of purpose! In most churches, the Sunday homily will last only about twelve minutes. That's just about enough time to put across one idea.

John Chrysostom could preach for an hour or more in a culture when people had the time to listen and expected a lengthy talk. As late as the nineteenth century, that was still common. In the pre-industrial milieu with no cell phones, cars, planes, TV, radio, or Internet, people had the leisure and patience for extended public speaking. A preacher could develop several ideas in such a situation.

In our age of the one-minute manager, however, shorter is better. The weekday homily is limited to three minutes so that many of the people can get to work on time — another reason for devotion to the one-idea homily.

Here, the "principle of three" helps:

- Tell them what you plan to say.
- Say it.
- Tell them what you told them.

I have witnessed a homilist take the three Sunday readings and dwell on the scriptural background for each one, discuss different life applications to be found in each reading, and try to link it all with what he spoke about last week — all in twelve minutes. He seemed blissfully unaware of the inability of the listeners to take in the diversity of images and comments, the disjointed material, and the confused result. Had he skillfully found a uniting theme for the three readings and drawn a credible application, his homily would have worked.

Adopt the artistry of the "power of one." A strong idea, presented with images, examples, and personal witness, engages the listeners and gives them something to think about.

When he became patriarch of Constantinople, he found a diocese with a badly managed budget, insufficient service for the poor, clerical laxity, and ostentatious hedonism among the rich. He corrected these abuses and filled his homilies with calls for conversion. His comments on the theater, aimed at the men in his congregation, have a contemporary ring:

> You get off balance when you meet a woman in the street. Then if you see a shameless woman in the theater, flaunting her soft sensuality, singing her immoral songs, throwing her limbs about in a dance, do you dare to say nothing happens to you? Long after the play those images float in your mind. You go home, not alone, but with the whore in your heart, kindling the Babylonian furnace.

Colorfully direct, Chrysostom added a sanction to his words:

> I announce in a loud voice: if any of you goes to the sinful outrages of the theater, I will not allow him back to this church, nor to approach the Holy Table. I will do as shepherds do, who separate the mangy sheep from the flock, lest they contaminate others.

He favored this confrontational style not just with his flock, but with errant priests and monks and absentee bishops, who preferred the excitement of the royal capitol to the dull routine of their rural dioceses. (I'm not sure that's the best approach today. I lean toward St. Francis de Sales, who drew listeners with "honey" rather than "vinegar.")

Of what use is it to weigh down Christ's table with golden cups, when he himself is dying of hunger? First fill him when he is hungry, then use the means you have left to adorn his table. What is the use of providing the table with cloths woven of gold thread and not providing Christ himself with the clothes he needs? . . . Do not therefore adorn the church and ignore your afflicted brother, for he is the most precious temple of all.

— JOHN CHRYSOSTOM, LITURGY OF THE HOURS, VOL. IV, P. 183

- Keep raising the bar for better homilies, like St. Paul.
- Derive homiletic courage from John Chrysostom on moral issues.
- Adopt the artistry of making only one point in your homilies.
- Call people to faith in Jesus Christ, who is revealing himself to us.
- Make faith growth in Christ the basis for bridging faith and life.

Chrysostom was a moralizer in the better sense of the word. He was no clerical hypocrite. He was incorrupt, courageous, and able to live what he preached. He did not just rage against sexual sins but the whole range of the seven capital sins. He also upheld the positive message of salvation and the power of faith.

In our culture, we are challenged by an increasing number of moral issues, both those brought into play by our modern "culture of death" and the perennial topics of injustice, the needs of the poor, and the problem of pain. To have the wisdom, balance, and courage needed to preach on these matters, we need to turn to Christ's love for us, a love that Chrysostom saw in St. Paul and in his own heart:

> Enjoying Christ's love, he (St. Paul) considered himself happier than anyone else. Were he without it, there would be no satisfaction to be the friend of principalities and powers. He preferred to be thus loved and to be the least of all. . . . As for tyrannical rulers or the people enraged against him, he paid them no more heed than gnats.
> — LITURGY OF THE HOURS, *OP. CIT.* P. 1323

The Call to Faith

In my first chapter, I identified the first duty of a homilist, which is to preach God's Word — another name for revelation. The second responsibility of a homilist is to call the listeners to faith in the God who speaks to us. The dynamic of revelation and faith response is the dialogue of salvation. Treat the invitation to faith as the context for your homilies. Note the insistence of recent popes on the need for evangelization. Paul VI wrote that the gap between faith and the culture is a tragedy of our time. He urges us to bridge this gap.

I agree, but would add that people need help first in appreciating how faith is originally a response to God's coming to meet us with love and salvation. God is in search of us. We are born to hunger for God. Our encounter with God is through faith, in which we joyfully surrender ourselves to the Lord.

I have always been intrigued with the way Billy Graham finishes all his sermons. Having delivered his perennial message about human sinfulness, the need for a savior, and the capacity to repent and believe in Jesus as savior, Graham invariably has an "altar call" — an invitation to walk the talk, to journey from the stands to the field in front of him and make a faith commitment to Jesus. It is only a beginning (or a return) of course, but a necessary one.

It is difficult to bridge the gap between faith and culture when we have not first crossed the threshold of hope, knelt in faith before Christ, and accepted his love. Jesus looks for us, and we search for him. When we meet, revelation links with faith. Being filled with his transforming love, we start to understand how faith opens us to the strength we need to live the faith in daily life.

Homilists with flourishing faith lives of their own will thread the summons to faith often in homilies — not always with those exact words, but each time, arousing faith in some sense. Some homilists frame their exhortations around culture of life issues; others choose the social justice ones. I believe both types need to integrate the nurturing of faith as an authentic "yes" to Jesus Christ, as well as a way to translate the Gospel for practical application.

Keep improving your standards for preaching, as did St. Paul. Draw inspiration from St. John Chrysostom's courage in preaching morality. Invite people to faith as a response to revelation. Draw the link between faith and culture.

In my homilies, how have I been calling people to faith?

God, help me to realize how much I need you.

Anyone who is kind to the poor lends to the Lord.

— Prov. 19:17

THREE

Begin with a Story

St. Ambrose dramatizes Scripture (339–397)

As the sounds of Ambrose's hymns flowed into my ears, truth was distilled into my heart.

— *Confessions, 9, 6*

I would be stretching credibility to imply that Ambrose sang during his homilies; that said, however, he was a homilist who also happened to be a singer, and a poet who composed hymns. Once people sang one of his hymns a few times, the simple and the learned both knew it by heart. His songs touched the feelings as well as the mind and were excellent teaching devices to counter the false instruction of the Arians.

Ambrose of Milan was raised in a prominent family that prized education. He was a trained lawyer and a born leader and became a consul. In 374, he was chosen Bishop of Milan by acclamation. He converted St. Augustine, fought the Arians, celebrated virginity, preached powerfully, and became a Father of the Church. St. Monica liked his homilies so much that she said, "That man is an angel."

The first thing I notice about his homilies is how clear they are. He visualizes the biblical scenes and stays close to the concrete circumstances. He displays his gift as a storyteller by looking at a given biblical narrative with the eye of a dramatist. Look how he breaks open the scene when Mary meets Elizabeth:

> Elizabeth is the first to hear Mary's voice, but John is the first to be aware of grace. She hears with the ears of the body, but he leaps for joy at the meaning of the mystery. She is aware of Mary's presence, but he is aware of the Lord's. . . . The women speak of the grace they have received while the children are active in secret unfolding the mystery of love with the help of their mothers, who prophesy by the Spirit of their sons.
>
> — Liturgy of the Hours, Vol. I, p. 353–4

Preach the Moral Virtues

Ambrose's familiarity with the Latin classics influenced his moral preaching, especially the value of the cardinal virtues of prudence, justice, temperance, and fortitude. Cicero and others had already recommended the need to practice these virtues in order to be moral. The spin — if I may use this term — that Ambrose brought to the topic was that these virtues were already celebrated in the Wisdom of Solomon (Wis. 8:7). He even hinted, perhaps humorously, that the Hebrews developed these virtues before the Romans did. Ambrose situated the cardinal virtues in a scriptural context by drawing examples from biblical figures.

The list of these four virtues was not enough for him. He added faith, hope, and charity as equally needed. This expansive idea is echoed by stone medallions of the cardinal virtues on the floor of Christ Church Cathedral in Oxford, where the traditional four virtues are crowned by the medallion "mercy." Christians believe that more virtues were required for morality. With a preacher's practicality, Ambrose illustrates the basic discipline used to acquire a virtue:

> A man wishing to undergo a warlike training daily exercises himself with his weapons. As though ready for action he rehearses his part in the fight and stands just as if the enemy were in position before him. The man that desires to navigate a ship on the sea, or to row, tries first on a river. They who wish to acquire an agreeable style of singing and a beautiful voice begin by bringing out their voice gradually by singing.
>
> — *On Duties*, X, 32

- Visualize the Gospel scene or the one from the Old Testament.
- Strive to be simple, clear and direct.
- Start with a story that captures the lesson of Scripture and relates it to the assembly.
- Illustrate your ideas with stories and examples.
- Choose stories from your life that taught you a lesson.

Still, Ambrose did not propose a spiritual athleticism devoid of grace. In his homilies on the Sacraments of Initiation, he reminds us that already in Baptism we receive the seven gifts of the Holy Spirit to help us gain the cardinal virtues. Devotion to God leads us to a holy life and motivates us to practice virtues.

Start Your Homily with a Story

The Church Fathers, including Ambrose, do not seem to start their homilies with a story. (Or, if they did so, the secretaries did not think it important to record them.) I have surmised that the Fathers did ease into their talks with stories, but the secretaries declined to record them, or they were told not to.

On the other hand, Jesus often began his talks with a story — a parable — usually followed by a life application. Sometimes, he just told a story and let its dramatic impact sink in. Jesus also used a number of metaphors, comparisons drawn from the rural life of his listeners. I have already shown how Ambrose could dramatize a scriptural scene with a touch of originality, and how he could list a string of examples to illustrate the effort to gain a virtue.

Though we do not think of Augustine as a storyteller, his *Confessions* is one of the greatest stories ever written, packed with spiritual lessons. I am a strong supporter of using stories in homilies, especially to start them. Surely, every homilist must know how difficult it is to get the attention of our listeners. The easiest way to do it is to tell a story that is pertinent to the Scripture lesson and the message we have prepared for the day.

This past summer, I attended a crowded Mass at a beach resort, accompanied by my hosts, a couple who generally went to church at a university parish. The homilist was animated and prepared and did not preach from the lectern. But later, as we compared notes, they echoed my own impression: the homily was too abstract. There were no stories or examples drawn from everyday life. I heard later that he had been a businessman prior to becoming a priest — yet he did not draw on his life experiences to illustrate his point.

A great deal has been written about the decline of religious literacy among Catholics. I have heard college religion teachers lament the

PREPARING YOUR SUNDAY HOMILY

1. Begin on Monday. Review readings for next Sunday. Mull them over in prayer each day. This is sometimes called The Divine Reading (*Lectio Divina*). Look up what scriptural commentaries say about the religious and cultural background and meaning of the texts. The Scottish minister William Barclay's commentaries are especially helpful (except for material about sacraments, Mary, saints, and the Pope). The late Bishop Untener liked to meet with some parishioners and other priests in a "Homily Committee" each week to review and pray over the readings, or to evaluate and correct planned homilies for the following Sunday.

2. By Thursday or Friday, many find it helpful to write out the homily. This clarifies your thinking — focuses on your goal or point. (See Chapter 14 for more on this recommendation.)

3. Make a detailed outline. Ask yourself:
   a. What do you want to say?
   b. Does your story fit the readings and your one point?
   c. Do you know how you will end? A pilot of a plane needs to know where, and how, he will land.

4. Saturday, make a smaller outline. Then make a *very* small outline. The smaller the outline, the better you know what you want to say, and the more you will use your own words — speak from your heart — and not memorized ones. The principle here is: move from words to ideas. If you know the idea you want to communicate, the words will come to you at the time of preaching. (I repeat this suggestion again, in a different context, in Chapter 14.)

absence of basic doctrinal knowledge in their students. Even Protestants are worried about the loss of familiarity with the Bible that was once so characteristic of their training. We no longer have a prevalent Christian culture to count on, as we could in times past. Granting the truth of this, a Scripture-based, doctrinally sound, liturgically apt homily may fall flat if the allusions mean little to a growing congregation bereft of the basics. In this situation, stories, illustrations, and examples are even more critical in explaining the Scripture text and the truths of faith.

If a homily is a club sandwich, the bacon and turkey are the teaching; the tomato, lettuce, and mayo are the "tastemakers" that spice it up and make it memorable; and the bread is the story/example that enables listeners to "carry the meat" of the teaching into their daily lives. Every idea needs a picture to stick to the ribs of the listeners — stories, stories, stories, free as the air you breathe. Some of the best come from your own reading and personal experiences, especially those that taught you important lessons. This is worth remembering, so we'll talk more about stories periodically throughout this book.

What have been the best stories you have used in homilies?

Dear God, show me how to tell your story of salvation.

Hearing is believing, but a word picture helps.

FOUR

Study the Bible

Ignorance of Scripture is ignorance of Christ.

— St. Jerome (340–420)

I know that priests and deacons can rarely be single-minded about studying Scripture the way that St. Jerome did, but his story can motivate the resolve to get closer to Scripture. All the Fathers of the Church loved the Bible and demonstrated this in their homilies. Jerome's specialty was Scripture itself.

Divine Providence gave him the talent for languages and the grace to use it. Born in Croatia, he was sent by his father to Rome for studies of Latin and Greek, baptized at eighteen, and experienced a second conversion at thirty. He joined a desert monastery outside of Antioch where, for four years, he studied Hebrew from a monk who converted from Judaism. About the difficulties of his Hebrew studies, he wrote:

> I turned to this hissing and broken winded language.
> What a labor it cost me! What difficulties I went through!
> How often I despaired and left off. Then started again. I thank
> God I now gather such sweet fruit from the bitter sowing of this seed.

He completed his formal study of Scripture from the masterful St. Gregory Nazianzen, then returned to Rome, where he was honored by the pope with the commission to make a new Latin translation of the Bible. Eventually, he moved to Bethlehem, where he spent the rest of his life on this project. His wealthy patron, Paula, built one monastery for men and another for women. His translation, known as the Vulgate, endured until it was replaced 1500 years later.

Besides his towering competence in Scripture, he is remembered for being a bad-tempered man, quarrelsome, given to biting comments about others, and so on. But he was often filled with remorse at his behavior

Sometimes it takes a poet with a sense of humor to defuse the folly of a saint. The following stanza takes the sting from the bee.

God's angry man, his crotchety scholar,
was St. Jerome, the great name-caller,
who cared not a dime for the laws of libel,
and in his spare time, translated the Bible.
He served his master, though with complaint,
he wasn't a plaster sort of saint.

— From *The Love Letters of Phyllis McGinley*

and repented frequently. Da Vinci portrays him with a lion at his feet, tamed because Jerome had removed a thorn from its paw. Jerome holds a stone in his hand about to beat it against his heart in repentance. Pope Sixtus V, looking at this painting, remarked, "You do well to have carried that stone, for without it the Church would never have canonized you."

Guidelines for Interpreting Scripture

We who are called to preach homilies are reading and interpreting Scripture every day. I recommend a patient reading of *Dei Verbum* at least once every year. It is one of the most accessible of the Vatican II documents and, like Scripture itself, is an inspiring and soul-renewing document. The text reminds us that Christ commanded the apostles to preach the Gospel. How did they do it? What can we learn from their method?

It was done by the apostles who handed on, by the spoken word of their preaching, by the example they gave, by the institutions they established, by what they themselves had received — whether from the lips of Christ, from his way of life and works, or whether they had learned it at the prompting of the Holy Spirit; it was done by those apostles and other men associated with the apostles, who, under the inspiration of the same Holy Spirit, committed the message of salvation to writing.

— Dei Verbum, 7

The Scripture begins in a living situation — first, with the words and deeds of Jesus, then, with the apostles, who proclaim in their words and deeds what they learned from Jesus — and becomes written under the influence of the Spirit, so that it can be known for generations to come. The spoken word became the written word. So that the Gospel may be preserved in the Church, the apostles left bishops as their successors, endowed with their own teaching and interpreting authority.

For many of us, the truths of Scripture were first received in a living context of our family life, our first experiences of the parish church and the sacraments, and the moral and virtue training imparted to us. These experiences of faith laid the groundwork for the formal education that followed. To some extent we were living stones of the church before we had the language to explain it. I realize this is contradicted sadly in many families and other situations where such privileges have not been passed on. But for priests and deacons, this is made up for, and supplemented by, years of training. We have our own version of the lived experience of the apostles, though obviously in a far lower key. Still, the sacramental presence of Jesus in the Eucharist does seem to bring Nazareth, Capernaum, Galilee, and Jerusalem to our doors.

The *Catechism of the Catholic Church* provides homilists with three principles of interpretation of Scripture:

112 Be especially attentive "to the content and unity of the whole Scripture."
Despite the variety and differences of the books, the varieties of literary forms and the contrasts of the Old and New Testaments, there is an internal unity binding all the material due to the unity of God's loving plan to save us. That unity is focused on Jesus Christ our Savior, who is the center and heart of all Scripture. All Scripture may be summed up in the preparation for the Savior, and the account of his appearance and fulfillment of all that was promised.

113 Read the Scripture within "the living Tradition of the whole Church."
The Fathers of the Church tell us that Sacred Scripture is written more in the *Church's heart* than in the written documents, essential and sacred though they are. The Church carries in her Tradition the living memorial of God's Word. At the same time, our search for the meaning of

the texts should be as broad as the history of the Church itself, looking at the Fathers and other scholars of the Church: medieval, Counter-Reformation, and contemporary. The lives of the saints from every period are living interpretations of Scripture. Think for a moment about when St. Thérèse of Lisieux was meditating on St. Paul and came to the realization that, through the text, God was calling her "to be Love in the heart of the Church."

114 Be attentive to the analogy of faith.

God is truth, so the divine truth that permeates Scripture is such that its earthly expressions are coherent among themselves. Taken together, they express the plan of salvation and help us to see the connections between them.

Another guideline is the two meanings of the text — the literal and the spiritual. We are called to determine the literal meaning as far as possible. Then, as we explore the spiritual meaning, the literal meaning provides a valuable foundation to build on.

While we recall the feisty personality of Jerome, we need to look at his tender side as well. In 404, Rome was sacked, and refugees flooded the Mediterranean world, including Bethlehem. Here is what Jerome wrote about the effect of that catastrophe:

> Who would have believed that the daughters of that mighty city would one day be wandering as servants and slaves on the shores of Egypt and Africa? That Bethlehem would daily receive noble Romans, distinguished ladies brought up in wealth and now reduced to beggary? I cannot help them all, but I grieve and weep with them. I am completely given over to the duties of charity. I have put aside my commentary on Ezechiel and all study. Today we must translate the words of scripture into deeds, and instead of speaking saintly words, we must act them.

> — *Butler's Lives of the Saints*, Vol. III, p. 692

- Continue your prayerful study of Scripture.
- Remember that "ignorance of Scripture is ignorance of Christ."
- Appreciate the unity of the Bible.
- Interpret Scripture in the whole Tradition of the Church,
- Use both the literal and spiritual meanings of Scripture.

In the post-Vatican II period, a number of outstanding American scholars helped us to gain a new and fruitful appreciation of Scripture, especially for our preaching. The trinity of Passionist congregation scholars — Barnabas Ahern, Carroll Stuhlmiller, and Donald Senior — are excellent tutors for our preaching God's Word. The outstanding contribution of Raymond Brown, especially his two-volume commentary on the Gospel of John, puts all of us in his debt. Among Protestant scholars, many of us enjoy the remarkable commentaries of William Barclay, filled with loads of cultural background and, in most cases, his canny Scot's practical applications. (More suggested materials are listed in the appendix of this book.)

If we follow the ancient practice of the monastic orders in the *Lectio Divina*, we have a daily path toward a faith- and prayer-based attitude to Scripture. This is a wholesome counterpart to our studies, so that they do not become separated from a relationship with God, whose word we ponder.

What is my approach to the study of Scripture?

Lord God, keep me faithful to the study of your holy word.

Don't be an empty preacher of God's Word because you no longer hear God in your heart.

— cf. *Dei Verbum*, 25

CHAPTER FIVE

Preach Christ

St. Leo the Great: defender of the Incarnation (400?–461)

For I decided to know nothing among you except Jesus Christ and him crucified.

— 1 COR. 2:2

When we attempt to understand the mystery of Christ's nativity, in which he was born of the Virgin Mother, let the clouds of earthly reasonings be driven far away, and the smoke of worldly wisdom be purged from the eyes of illuminated faith. For the authority by which we believe is divine, and divine is the teaching which we follow.

— ST. LEO THE GREAT
(*FAITH OF THE EARLY FATHERS*, VOL. 3; WILLIAM A. JURGENS,
LITURGICAL PRESS, COLLEGEVILLE, MN, P. 276)

Leo the Great served as pope for twenty-one years. Around him, the Roman Empire declined and officially collapsed in 476. But as imperial Rome faded, Christian Rome ascended. Leo is the first pope from whom a large body of homilies survived, just a little over 100. Of all the papal homilies available to us, Leo's are a marvel of clarity, sharpness, and even rhythmic prose.

Politically, he is famous for stopping Attila the Hun from savaging Rome and, later, convincing Gaiseric the Vandal to spare Rome from fire, torture, and massacre (though the barbarian did loot the city).

Theologically, he asserted, in teaching and practice, the authority of the Bishop of Rome as the successor of St. Peter over the universal Church. When the Fathers of the Council of Chalcedon approved of Canon 28, elevating the See of Constantinople to the same patriarchal status as Rome, Leo vigorously rejected that decision and affirmed the primacy of the See of Peter in Rome.

But his greater energies, theologically, were spent on clarifying and supporting the doctrine of the Incarnation, as formulated by the Council of Nicea: the two natures of Christ, divine and human, united in the Person of the Word made flesh. He fully supported the calling of the Fourth General Council, held at Chalcedon in 451, where the Fathers approved his position on Christ, recognizing his teaching as the "voice of Peter." The liturgy of the Church has adopted Leo's homilies on the birth of Jesus for both Christmas and Epiphany.

Deeds, Not Creeds?

Some people claim that today we should preach about "deeds" more than "creeds." This assumes that there are no challenges to Christian doctrines, but plenty of assaults on social and individual moral issues. I would agree that we have a number of moral problems to preach about — but the creeds need our attention as well as the deeds, especially since the true nature of Christ is being undermined.

The Jesus Seminar skillfully used the media to argue that Jesus is not God. For a while, the Christmas and Easter cover stories of the major news magazines carried the message of the Seminar into the homes of America. A number of the new mega-churches appear to have little in the way of creeds. Many of them even eliminate the title Christian or Church and simply call themselves "communities." Their religious services seem to put little stress on the worship of God or the moral and doctrinal requirements of traditional Christianity.

New Age advocates call for the separation of spirituality from religion. This is presented as liberation from the discomforting traits of religion — beliefs to be held, rituals to be followed at worship, or moral laws to be obeyed. Even Christmas has come under fire, with local laws against Nativity cribs on public property, and salespersons and restaurant service people greeting us with "Happy Holidays" instead of "Merry Christmas." The supporters of these changes argue, ironically enough, that they are being "inclusionary"; they fail to see either the humor or the illogic in *excluding* Christian observations in order to be *inclusive*.

In 1931, Fulton J. Sheen wrote the book *Old Errors, New Labels,* in which he identified the persistence of doctrinal errors that reappear in new and beguiling forms. During the first five centuries of the Church — including New Testament times — there were repeated efforts to change the truth about Christ. The Gnostics denied he was human. Later, the Arians denied he was divine. Both groups found a number of ways to insinuate their ideas into mainstream Christianity, often with alarming success. Their fundamental objection was that it was unacceptable to imagine or believe that God could become human. It was unfitting for the dignity of God to be limited by the restrictions of being human. Indeed, the very idea was humiliating. St. Paul answered this idea in the second chapter of Philippians, where he dwells on the humility of God. The self-humbling of God was a divine answer to the self-inflated pride of humans who overestimated themselves.

Among the many books that are helpful for preaching Christ, I recommend the just-quoted Guardini book, *The Lord*, as being one of the most original and insightful reflections on the Life of Christ. I also find Archbishop Sheen's *Life of Christ* to be filled with vivid scenes from the Gospels, inspiringly written. Also, I have drawn homiletic ideas from Franco Zeferelli's eight-hour film, *Jesus of Nazareth*, available on VHS or DVD.

Romano Guardini responded to all those who cannot accept the union of the divinity and humanity in Christ, not with the usual language of person and nature, but with a discussion of the humility of God. It was an ingenious approach, since he struck at the human cause of the disbelief:

> Man is not a noble being, not a beautiful soul or exalted spirit, but a sinner — *peccator*. And as if this were not enough, a sinner in the eyes of a humble judge. Here we have it, expression of profoundest revolt in the often heard words, God is not to my taste. Humility means the breaking of this satanic taste reaction, the bowing deeply not only before God's majesty, but even more deeply before his humility. . . . It means that as a natural human being, conscious of health, beauty, strength, talent, intelligence and culture, he submits to him who from these familiar standards seems so questionable: Christ on the Cross.

— Romano Guardini, *The Lord*, p. 328

Another superb book about Christ is Blessed Columba Marmion's *Christ the Life of the Soul*. It's a unique blend of Scripture, liturgy, and spirituality.

Dominus Jesus

In 1985, Paul Knitter published his paperback *No Other Name?*, in which he wrote that the Logos-Word was not only incarnate in Jesus, but also in other founders of world religions, such as Mohammed, Buddha, Krishna, and so on. The title of his book was taken from Acts 4:12, in which Peter confesses before the Sanhedrin the origin of his ministry and miracles:

> "And there is salvation in no one else, *for there is no other name under heaven* given among men by which we must be saved."
>
> (emphasis added)

Knitter puts a question mark after "no other name," to indicate he believes there are other saviors in whom the Logos dwelt.

On August 6, 2000, the Congregation of the Doctrine of the Faith published *Dominus Jesus*, in which the uniqueness of Jesus as the only Savior was explained and defended. In paragraphs 9 and 10, the document describes positions opposed to the Lord Jesus as the only Savior and incarnation of the Logos.

> 9. In contemporary theological reflection there often emerges an approach to Jesus of Nazareth that considers him a particular, finite, historical figure, who reveals the divine not in an exclusive way, but in a way complementary with other revelatory and savior figures. The Infinite, the Absolute, the Ultimate mystery of God would thus manifest itself to humanity in many ways and many historical figures: Jesus of Nazareth would be one of these. More, concretely, for some, Jesus would be one of the many faces which the Logos has assumed in the course of time to communicate with humanity in a salvific way. . . .
>
> 10. These theses are in profound conflict with the Christian faith. The doctrine of faith must be *firmly believed* which proclaims that Jesus of Nazareth, son of Mary, and he alone is the Son, and the Word of the Father.
>
> (SEE: JN. 1:14; MT. 16:16; JN. 1:18; COL. 1:13–14, 19–20)

To indicate any separation between the Word and Jesus Christ is unacceptable. It is also contrary to the Catholic faith to introduce a capacity to be a Savior to anyone other than Jesus Christ, the only Savior and Lord. The text of *Dominus Jesus* cites numerous Scripture texts, as well as conclusions of Councils, to explain and defend the divinity and humanity of Christ, as well as his being the unique and only Savior of the world. See especially paragraphs 9–15.

I draw this document to your attention because it is readable and preachable for homilies about the mystery of Christ — along with the text from Acts 4:12, as well as Peter's two confessions of the mystery of Jesus: "You are the Christ, the Son of the living God" (Mt. 16:16) and "Lord, to whom shall we go? You have the words of eternal life" (Jn. 6:68).

I conclude this reflection on preaching Christ with the words of an old evangelical hymn filled with faith in the uniqueness of Jesus, the solid rock of our salvation.

CHRIST, THE SOLID ROCK – LK. 6:43–49

My hope is built on nothing less
Than Jesus' blood and righteousness.
I dare not trust the sweetest frame,
But wholly lean on Jesus' Name.

Refrain
On Christ, the solid rock, I stand.
All other ground is sinking sand.
All other ground is sinking sand.

When darkness hides his lovely face,
I rest on his unchanging grace.
Through every high and stormy gale
My anchor holds within the veil. (**Refrain**)

Words: Edward Mote · Music: William Bradbury
(As recorded by Benny Hester, © Word Music, LLC.
All rights reserved. Used by permission.)

What do I consider my best homilies about Jesus Christ?

Jesus, teach me how to preach you.

"Worthy is the Lamb who was slain, to receive power and wealth and wisdom and might and honor and glory and blessing!"

— Rev. 5:12

SIX

Welcome the New Evangelization

St. Gregory the Great (540–604): creating Christian Europe

I cannot preach with any competence, and yet insofar as I do succeed, still I myself do not live my life according to my own preaching.

— GREGORY THE GREAT, FROM HIS *HOMILY ON EZECHIEL*

Born of old Roman stock and given the best education, Gregory was immensely gifted. He had the soul of a monk and turned his family mansion into a monastery. Popes kept appointing him to active posts, drawing him away from his beloved monastic life. In 590 he was elected Pope. Because of the collapse of the empire of the west, Gregory assumed much of the leadership, both temporal and spiritual. He used the papal treasuries to relieve social distress, fostered civic organization to overcome chaos, and negotiated peace with the invading tribes.

Gregory not only had the soul of a monk; he also possessed the spirit of a missionary. His most successful mission effort was his sending Augustine and forty monks to England to establish a monastery at Canterbury in 596. Later, in 601, he sent reinforcements led by Melitus and Paulinus, who eventually became bishops of York and London. He conferred the pallium on Augustine as first archbishop of Canterbury, which became the Catholic heart of England until the Reformation.

His support for the spread of monastic life had the effect of rooting the faith in Western Europe, the civilizing of the tribes and stabilizing their nomadic impulses. Historian Christopher Dawson wrote of this as *The Making of Europe*. This was an evangelization that had both spiritual and temporal results. Gregory's book, *Pastoral Care*, became the textbook for how to be a bishop, and was in use for centuries. His 62 surviving homilies have an evangelizing tone. He was one of the most influential popes in history and is correctly called "The Great."

The New Evangelization

I was surprised recently when a middle-aged priest asked me, "What is evangelization?" I said it means saying yes to Jesus Christ, to his call for repentance, to his offer of salvation, to his teachings, and to active membership in his Church, which includes active participation in the sacraments and witnessing Christ in our lives. He still looked puzzled and said, "What do evangelizers do?" I replied that they try to get others to say yes to the option for Christ I had briefly described. He nodded and said no more.

I thought he might then ask, "What is the New Evangelization?" He didn't, but many others ask me that. It is an expression popularized by

Here are Gregory's self-deprecating thoughts about his difficulties in preserving inner peace and thoughts about God amid so many pastoral demands. Today's busy deacons and priests may be consoled by his frank comments about his shortcomings.

> Since I assumed the burden of pastoral care, my mind can no longer be collected; it is concerned with so many matters. I must weigh the lives and acts of individuals. I am responsible for the concerns of our citizens. I must worry about the roving bands of barbarians, and beware of the wolves who lie in wait for my flock. . . . I must put up with certain robbers without losing patience and at times I must deal with them in all charity. With my mind divided and torn to pieces by so many problems, how can I meditate or preach wholeheartedly without neglecting the ministry of proclaiming the Gospel. . . . At times I let my tongue run. . . . As a result I often listen patiently to chatter. And because I too am weak, I find myself drawn little by little into idle conversation, and I begin to talk freely about matters which once I would have avoided. What once I find tedious, I now enjoy.

> — Liturgy of the Hours, Vol. IV, p. 1366

Pope John Paul II. He spoke of it as "new" in the sense that the situation in which it happens is new. For example, bringing Christ to those who do not know him is more daunting than ever.

> The number of those who do not know Christ has doubled since the end of Vatican II. When we consider the immense portion of humanity whom the Father loves and for whom he has sent his Son, the urgency of the Church's mission is obvious.
>
> — MISSION OF THE REDEEMER (RM), 3.2

Another new quality of evangelization is addressing the de-Christianization of formerly Christian countries. Such countries need to be re-evangelized.

The third new aspect of evangelization is what Pope John Paul called the contemporary forms of the Areopagus, where St. Paul preached at Athens. Its modern forms are:

(1) The new forms of mass communication with which we are familiar. When he spoke to the 500 leaders of the media at the Sheraton Universal Studios in 1987, Pope John Paul asked them to be conscious of the universal moral values that promote human dignity, rights, and duties in their productions, attitudes, and forms of communication. He was basically evangelizing them at a level they could immediately grasp. The Church needs to use these new "Roman roads" to bring the Gospel to the global village.

(2) The second area is an agenda for evangelizing homilies: commitment to peace, development and liberation of peoples, the rights of individuals and peoples, especially minorities, the advancement of women and children, and safeguarding the created world. These areas need to be enlightened by the Gospel (RM 37.13).

(3) The third new area where evangelization calls us to shed the light of Christ is the world of scientific research, which is raising numerous moral questions. This is fascinating and challenging for the homilist.

Though materialism seems rampant, there is also a new search for meaning, a desire to know about one's inner life, a desire to be taught

"Your homily changed my life."

A priest friend of mine had a woman tell him this. She went on to say, "My father died fifteen years ago, when I needed him most. It shook my faith and left me depressed. I kept asking God 'Why did you let that happen?' Two weeks ago you said that the 'why' question may not be helpful in dealing with pain of loss. The answer is seldom satisfying. Better to ask God 'how' to get on with my life and my relationship with him. You removed a cloud from my mind and a burden from my heart."

An evangelizing homily evokes the possibility of change.

how to pray better and to be instructed in the paths of meditation. There is a religious revival occurring, with possibilities and shortcomings. We would be wise to adopt it as an opportunity to put an evangelizing tone into our homilies. This is not an attempt to impose anything, but rather to propose the option for love, the option for Jesus Christ and all he means for humanity.

If you want to get a sense of how the new evangelization would impact your homilies, I recommend a prayerful reading of *The Mission of the Redeemer*. If you read only paragraphs 36 and 37, it is worth your time.

Some Wise Advice

One of the wisest evangelizers of our time was the late Paulist Fr. Alvin Illig, the founder of the Paulist National Catholic Evangelization Association (202/832-5022; Web site: www.pncea.org). I cite their phone number and URL because the organization remains a vital pastoral resource for the new evangelization in the United States.

Fr. Illig was an experienced evangelizing homilist who developed a number of practical ideas on how to do it, some of which I cite here:

1. Consider Christ's Great Commission to evangelize (Mt. 28:18–20) as a spiritual vocation contained in our baptismal,

confirmation and ordination commitment. Jesus gives us the vocation. We must develop the method. Take heart in the knowledge that God who wills the end also wills the means. God will help you to find the right means.

2. Be positive and hope-filled. As God's messengers and real Easter homilists, believe you have Good News to share with others. Announce God's kingdom of love, justice and mercy. (Cf. Lk. 4:43)

3. Adopt a friendly attitude. Work with Pope John XXIII's maxims:
    "We come not to conquer. We come to serve."
    "Offer people the medicine of Christ's mercy."

4. Look beyond the brick and mortar. Look instead at the time, talent and treasure of your people.

5. Evangelize yourself through daily spiritual renewal and union with Christ. Convinced people convince others. Preach what you practice, as well as practicing what you preach.

6. Don't wait for a perfect Church or a perfect life. Be a witness to Christ in your present state of growth and the Church's present stage of her journey. We will always be sinners being saved and the weak being strengthened.

7. Do your best, and leave the rest to God.

How would you make your homilies more evangelizing?

Jesus, show me how to evangelize.

I am eager to preach the Gospel.
— Rom. 1:15

SEVEN

Say the Idea — Speak a Picture

St. Thomas Aquinas (1225–1274): the marriage of reason and faith

I think many would be surprised to know that when Thomas Aquinas became a Master of Theology at the University of Paris, his principal responsibility was to preach the Word of God. The professors of the time regarded the breaking open of the Scriptures one of their most important tasks. They felt called to change lives and form hearts and move people to salvation. Thomas fulfilled his preaching task with his customary depth and in the light of his extensive commentaries on the Bible.

> Thomas's principal academic responsibility was not to lecture in philosophy or metaphysics or even systematic theology, but rather to illumine and explain the sacred page of scripture. It is interesting — and highly regrettable — that among Aquinas's least known works are his biblical commentaries, precisely those presentations that were, at least in principle, at the very heart of his project. Aquinas scholars are discovering only today the scriptural "feel" and focus in all of his more formally theological tracts.
>
> — ROBERT BARRON, *THOMAS AQUINAS — SPIRITUAL MASTER*,
> CROSSROADS, NY, 1996, PP. 20–21

Of course, Aquinas also was a major professor of philosophy and theology, especially presiding over the customary debates about disputed questions. In his writings, especially in the *Summa*, he recovered many of the thousands of objections and replies that marked his years in the classroom. I believe you would find Fr. Barron's approach to Aquinas as a spiritual master a compelling interpretation of Thomas's works. In his view, the first part of the Summa describes God's "ecstasy," that is, his divine outpouring of love in creation and for all people. In part three, the perfect response to this love is in the incarnate Word, Jesus Christ, whose "ecstasy" is an outpouring of love in return — through his redeeming

> God's self-disclosure was necessary for "human salvation." God does not reveal himself in order to illumine our minds or satisfy our curiosity. Rather God does so in order to move us, to shake us, to push us outside of and beyond ourselves in order to be saved.
>
> — Barron, 35

life, death, and resurrection for our salvation. Part two outlines the vices to be avoided and the virtues to be acquired in living out the redeemed life Jesus has acquired for us. Barron shows how this approach carries the writings of Aquinas beyond an abstract, uninvolved perspective to a concrete method for spiritual direction.

I would like to draw your attention to another point Thomas makes, one useful for preaching: there is nothing in the mind that was not first in the senses. He rooted his teachings in the concrete order before ascending to other heights. This was his first step in the process of knowing. His modern disciple, Bernard Lonergan, outlined this process in four stages of knowing. For myself, I have simplified these steps and applied them to the preaching act, which I think you may find helpful.

Four Steps in Knowing ... applied to the homiletic process

Sensation

There is nothing in the mind that was not first in the senses of touch, smell, taste, sight, and sound. Homilists should begin with the world as it is. This is being "down to earth (*humus*)," a humble attitude in communication. It is a call to be incarnational, like the Son of God who emptied himself of the status of glory and assumed the earthly form of human nature. People admire preachers who have the "common touch." This is the rationale for using stories, word pictures, images, and poems as homily starters, as well as other illustrations within the homily. That is the meaning of my axiom, "Say the idea — Speak a picture." See this as common "sense." Think of beginning a homily at the point that human knowing starts — at the level of sensation. Sustain that method using your imagination.

LEARNING THROUGH OUR SENSES

We can listen to lectures, read books, see films and slides, and talk to travelers, but nothing can compare with actually going there ourselves. Then, we can absorb impressions by all five senses. We see the Lake of Galilee and the undulating hills of Samaria with our own eyes. We hear the noise of bargaining in the market place and the bleating of a mixed flock of sheep and goats. We touch an old gnarled olive tree, or let the waters of the River Jordan trickle through our fingers. We taste the juice of the grapes of Israel or the sweetness of a fig or orange or pomegranate. We smell the scent of the flowers of the field. And the whole Bible comes alive! We have discovered the land for ourselves.

— John Stott, *Between Two Worlds*.
Grand Rapids, MI: Eerdmans, 1982, p. 79

Imagination

The mind takes the products of the senses and forms inner pictures. This occurs in our imaginations. The imagination makes pictures out of what is sensed. It is also able to mix and match these impressions and create new combinations. Storytellers, novelists, poets, and even scientists benefit from this capacity of the imagination. I include scientists who themselves testify to the power of imagination to get themselves outside the box and beyond the routine. It is what prompts them to discover and to shout, "Eureka!" As homilists, you can nurture your imagination by reading poetry and literature. The Psalms are a gold mine of scriptural pictures that stimulate the imagination as well as prayer. Great works of art and films are imagination starters and sustainers. Once you gain a respect for your imagination, you can begin to see its power for preaching.

Abstraction

The mind takes the steps of sensation and imagination and forms concepts and ideas. At this stage the process of knowing deals with the

> I am enough of an artist to draw freely upon my imagination. Imagination is more important than knowledge. Knowledge is limited. Imagination circles the world. . . . The intuitive mind is a sacred gift and the rational mind is a faithful servant. We have created a society that honors the servant and has forgotten the gift.
>
> — Albert Einstein

heart of the matter, the essentials of things. This is the message stage of preaching. Here you deal with Scripture, doctrine, theology, philosophy, and catechesis. You need to recall that the ideas and concepts in these areas were the result of human experiences (sensations) and imagination that led to a particular aspect of knowing. Patriarchs, prophets, apostles, saints, and religious thinkers have gone through this process for centuries, aided by faith and grace. The knowledge received from the fields mentioned deepens and gives permanence to the religious message you plan to deliver.

Judgment

Now your mind takes sensations, imaginations, and concepts and makes a judgment on how to apply God's Word to your people in a given homily. This is the application stage of preaching. We have before us impressions, feelings, sense experiences, stories, images, pictures, and ideas. Now comes the "So what?" This is the moment of truth, the moral of your message, the challenge you wish to pose, the outcome of the process you have gone through. This is the "take home pay" for your listeners. People need deeds as well as creeds in the sense that Christian witness is the desired outcome of a homiletic exhortation. We are doing more than conducting a pleasant passage of twelve minutes of public speaking. We are involved in the spiritual formation of our listeners, a shaping of souls for the kingdom of God and the salvation of the world, with the help of the power of the Holy Spirit.

Judgment is the faculty of prudent application of the process of discernment described here. It works best if we have an attitude of faith, prayer, and humility. The prophets of the Bible frequently said, "The word

ST. DOMINIC AND HIS ORDER OF PREACHERS

St. Dominic was born in Caleruega, Spain, in 1170. After his studies in theology, he became a Canon of Osma. During a trip to southern France, he encountered the Albigensian heresy. He stayed in France and worked effectively against this heresy by preaching and good example. To help him with his work, he founded the Order of Preachers. He taught them the value and power of effective preaching based on God's truth found in Scripture and sacred doctrine. He urged them to study Scripture constantly. It was said he always carried with him the Gospel of Matthew and the epistles of Paul. His Order became associated with the new universities, where their brothers, St. Albert the Great and St. Thomas Aquinas, ranked among the greatest philosophers and theologians in Church history.

The relevance of Dominic and his Order remains today to face up to the new challenges of relativism, secularism, and religious indifference. They can use the same tools the early Order had: freedom from attachment to material goods, the conviction that preaching is a powerful means to overcome such evils, and the persistent study of divine and human truth.

of the Lord came to me." I would apply that saying to our homilies in the sense that an effective homily is a gift of the Holy Spirit, who hovers over our musings and presents us that holy gift. These four steps are not the only available descriptions of the process of knowing, but I find this one the most useful for preaching and trust you may find it so as well.

I would say that among the four steps of knowing, the first two are the most ignored. Awareness of the senses and the imagination keep us close to experience and intuition, a treasure house of material that makes our homilies accessible and persuasive. For most of us, our education has prized the absorption of knowledge and the acquisition of critical judgment, while underplaying experience and creativity. After a while, however, this is like putting up a building while forgetting the needed foundations. A return to the whole picture of the "knowing" process will yield better homilies.

What is the role of experience and imagination in my homilies?

Holy Spirit, grant me the gift of creativity.

A rock pile ceases to be a rock pile the moment a single man contemplates it, bearing within him the image of a cathedral.

— Antoine de Saint-Exupéry

EIGHT

Preaching about the Saints

St. Catherine of Siena . . . she changed the mind of a pope

To dwell above with the saints we love, that's a bit of glory.
To dwell below with saints we know, that's a different story.

— ANONYMOUS

History is a record of the "best of times and the worst of times," as Dickens expressed it. Historian Barbara Tuchman characterized the calamitous fourteenth century to be among the worst of times. The Black Death wiped out a third of Europe's population. The Hundred Years' War brutalized all the participants. The Avignon Papacy threatened to undermine the spiritual influence of the Church.

This was the woeful world into which Catherine of Siena was born. From an early age she demonstrated a strong attraction to mystical prayer. As a young adult, she became a member of the Third Order of the Dominicans; she dictated her visions to secretaries and engaged Dominican Friar Raymond of Capua to be her spiritual director and counselor.

She also visited prisoners, especially those on death row, whom she comforted on their way to execution, encouraging their faith in eternal life. She volunteered at the hospitals and provided food and clothing for the poor. As her reputation grew, she became an advisor to kings and princes.

Her greatest concern was the Avignon Papacy. She traveled to the papal city and stayed there for four months, intent on persuading Pope Gregory XI to move the papal household back to Rome. Virtually every day, she went to the papal court and tried any number of approaches to convince Gregory to change. Her importuning the Holy Father was a public affair at a time when the audience hall was open to all and sundry. What Catherine said, everyone heard.

With neither a hint of shyness nor the slightest evidence of being intimidated, Catherine used a forthright strategy with the pope. "Be a man, Father! Arise! Don't be negligent!" Sometimes she called him — of all things — *dolce babbo mio* (my sweet daddy). In a thousand ways, she stated her plan for the pope:

> Begin the reform of the Church through appointing worthy priests. Make peace with Florence, not by arms, but by pardon and mercy. Return to Rome, not with swords and soldiers, but with the Cross and the Blessed Lamb. O Father, peace, for the love of God.

What finally convinced Gregory was her clairvoyant declaration when she reminded him of a secret promise he had made. "Who knows God's will as well as your holiness, for did you not, when you were a cardinal, vow to yourself that if you were elected pope you would return the papacy to Rome?" That did it. Despite loud objections from the cardinals and enormous pressure from the French monarchy, Gregory set sail for Rome and restored the papacy to that city.

Catherine returned to Siena, where she died in her thirty-third year. Her last words were full of self-reproach that she had not loved Jesus as deeply as she knew was possible. No one agreed with her. Their "mamma" loved Christ more than any of them believed possible.

Against all odds for a woman of her time and station, Catherine rose to the center of international power and changed the course of Church history. She was not dealing with children, and they did not act that way. Pope Gregory permitted her endearing *"dolce babbo"* address, but he remained until the end the calculating, measured chief executive of the Church; he required four months of aggressive convincing by Catherine before he conceded. She relied on her visions and prayers as well as her tough-minded capacity to stay in there and negotiate. She was assertive in the best sense of the word. Because of that, the papacy and the Church are in her debt. Her statue in Rome is on the Via della Conciliazione, the street that opens out to St. Peter's — and Catherine's head is tilted, so that she still keeps an eye on the Holy Father.

Preaching the Saints

Because the memorials and feasts of saints are on weekdays, it is rare that a homilist will ever have much more than three to five minutes to say much about the saint of the day. The secret is to pick a colorful anecdote from the life of the saint that captures a virtue or wisdom saying that would be beneficial to the listeners. It is not a good idea, nor is there time normally, to indulge in telling the life story of the saint.

Choose a scene that tells a story instead.

When Vincent de Paul lay dying, a novice came to him and said, "What did you find was the best way to approach the poor?"

"My daughter," he replied, "you must love them for the bread you put into their hands. Humble yourself before them, so they will never feel you are patronizing them."

The moral of the story draws attention to the desired attitude for working with the poor.

A new sister in the Carmel of Lisieux wanted to know how to approach prayer. "Sr. Thérèse, how should I pray your little way?"

Thérèse advised her, "Imagine what you were like as a small child before you learned to read. Recall the simplicity of your heart in those days."

The young sister had another question. "What will I do when I feel dry at prayer?"

Thérèse told her, "Just take the Our Father and say one word at a time, allowing much silence in between the words. Drop each word into the well of your silence."

This would be an opportunity to repeat St. Thérèse's axiom, "God does not expect great deeds, only everyday acts done with great love."

Maria Goretti was twelve years old when Alessandro Serenelli attacked her, dragged her into the kitchen, and attempted to rape her. She fought him fiercely and told him that God forbade what he was doing. After failing to choke her into submission, he stabbed her fourteen times. She survived one day. When she gained consciousness, she saw a statue of Mary at the foot of her bed. She forgave Alessandro and prayed that he would join her in heaven.

During his years in prison, Alessandro repented after receiving a vision of Maria gathering lilies and handing them to him. In 1950, he was present at her canonization. Her courage is a message that purity and abstinence are not just possible, but can be blessed.

Near the end of his stay in the Tower of London, Thomas More was visited by his family, who urged him to submit to the King's divorce and takeover of the Church, and thus rescue the family's finances and reputation. He said no.

Then he looked at his wife Alice. "That's a nice dress you're wearing."

"Is it?"

"Alice, this custard is delicious."

"Is it? Thomas, I don't understand why you are doing this."

More replied in a broken voice, "But you must. I cannot make a good death unless you do."

"I know one thing," she shouted to the sky. "You're the best I've ever met or am likely to."

More hugged her. "Why, it's a lion I've married!"

So much is here in this little scene for a homily: personal integrity, marital love, fidelity to God. (Scene paraphrased from Robert Bolt, *A Man For All Seasons* Vintage Book. Random House, 1960, p. 83.)

Sources for Saints

What sources are available for homilists?

I keep Butler's four-volume *Lives of the Saints* on hand. He usually gives a lot more than you need, and his language is often heavy, but you can lighten it up and turn it into a dialogue.

I also like Woodeene Koenig-Bricker's excellent *365 Saints* (Harper), a book very helpful for the short weekday homily. She devotes one page to each saint and provides a moral of the story, plus a little question on how to apply the saint's message to one's life. For example, in her life of St. Louise de Marillac, Woodeene notes that this busy Daughter of Charity worried about the spiritual welfare of her son, Michael. Louise's biographer wrote, "With all her occupations, she never forgot Michael's needs." Then, Woodeene asks us, "Is there someone in my life I have neglected lately?"

Another source I use regularly is *Saints of the Roman Calendar* by Enzo Lodi (Alba House). For each saint, Lodi provides a short biography and a small reference to the liturgical history of the feast or memorial.

I admit it. I love the saints. I've loved them as long as I can remember. One of the first joys of my childhood was receiving a book about St. Francis of Assisi. (And one of my first great disappointments was not being chosen to play the role of St. Clare in our third grade production of St. Francis's life.) I can't imagine life without the saints. I don't know what I would do without St. Anthony to help find lost objects, or Blessed Diana D'Andalo to consult on maintaining friendships. I know my life would be diminished without a celestial shoulder to cry on or occasionally a heavenly companion to share an earthly joy.
— Woodeene Koenig-Bricker, *365 Saints: Your Daily Guide to the Wisdom and Wonder of Their Lives.* HarperSanFrancisco, 1995; Introduction

Then, he gives a fine application, which he calls "Message and Relevance." He generally bases his observations on the three prayers of the Mass, or sometimes from other parts of the Mass or from a homily given at the canonization.

Occasionally, films about saints can provide homily material. Certainly the film *Becket* offers a number of anecdotes about the conversion of Thomas Becket from political chancellor to saintly archbishop. The life of Thomas More in the magnificent film *A Man for all Seasons* is filled with a number of small scenes that can be adopted for a homily. I also think of *The Song of Bernadette* and *Brother Sun, Sister Moon*.

What helps me to give a good homily about a saint?

*Saints of God, pray for me for the wisdom I need
to preach Christ through you.*

Inquisitor: "Joan of Arc, do you consider yourself to be in the state of grace?"
Joan: "If I am not, may God put me there.
If I am, may God keep me there."

NINE

Marian Homilies

St. Bernard of Clairvaux (1090–1153)

D oes a person make history, or does history make the person? Someone answered this question by saying, "I'm not going to read history; I'm going to make it."

Academics in the nineteenth century supported the "great man" theory: it was the hero who shaped history. In the twentieth century, the
emphasis changed; now, history shaped the leader, who was tutored by
the social currents of the day. However, I wonder about this interpretation when I think of the epic leaders, both good and bad, who dominated the history of that bloody century. Still, there is a grain of truth in
each position. Heroes are products of their culture and express and ful-
fill their ambitions in the ethos of their times.

Such a man was Bernard of Clairvaux, who revived the faltering Cis-
tercian Order and made it prosper. He had the good fortune of becoming a leader in a medieval Europe that was arriving at its zenith, when
devotion to Mary was a symbol of the power of faith in society. As
numerous Gothic cathedrals dominated the skylines of Christendom,
they bore the name of Mary, Our Lady, *Notre Dame*. Bernard was her
court poet, her monastic knight, and her defender against all opposition. The marriage of one of history's greatest architectural achievements
with the gracious presence of the Queen of Heaven was ready-made for
Bernard's homiletic skills

Those who regularly pray the full Liturgy of the Hours get a taste of
the energy of Bernard's preaching, even though removed from him by
eight centuries. I particularly like his homily on the Annunciation, chosen for the Office of Readings on December 20. Bernard publicly talks to
Mary at the moment she has heard Gabriel's announcement that God is
asking her to be the mother of his Son. She had said she did "not know

man," seemingly indicating she had no plans for that. To this, Gabriel replies that the Holy Spirit would conceive the child in her.

She is now in a state of reflection, pondering an answer. Bernard enters into her silence and assumes the voice of the human race in need of the salvation — "We shall be free if you consent." He tells her that tearful Adam begs this; so do Abraham and David. All her ancestors urge her to say yes. Raising the ante, Bernard exclaims that the entire world waits upon her consent. Rhetorically, his homily still rings with drama for us every Advent. He presses his case:

> Answer quickly, O Virgin. Reply in haste to the angel, or rather through the angel to the Lord. Answer with a word, receive the Word of God. Speak your own word, conceive the divine Word. Breathe a passing word, embrace the eternal Word. Why do you delay? Why are you afraid? Believe, give, praise and receive. Let humility be bold, let modesty be confident. This is no time for virginal simplicity to forget prudence. In this matter alone, O prudent Virgin, do not fear to be presumptuous.
>
> — LITURGY OF THE HOURS, VOL. I, PP. 345–6

Once More — with Feeling

The soaring preaching of Bernard, boldly urging Mary to say yes to the Incarnation, exudes an intimacy we can only envy in our subdued and tentative times; it invites us to allow our hearts to surge with joy and holy impatience. Notice his creativity in building his homily out of an interval in the story when Mary silently prays over what her response to God should be. He imagines himself with her at this critical moment in salvation history and passionately argues for her consent.

Faith literally flares up from his heart. His was not an emotion designed to manipulate Mary or us, his listeners. His feeling was seamlessly bonded to his theology and faith.

Most of us are so understated in our proclamation of the Gospel that many wonder if we *have* a statement to make. Of course, we cannot and should not fake feeling, nor ought we be maudlin. But even if we choose to speak "under the radar," it can be with a drive, an energy, a passion, that wakes up souls and thrills them with God's presence and Mary's intercessions. I recall a line from Morris West's novel *Daughter of Silence*,

WHAT RULES DO I FOLLOW FOR MY HOMILIES ON MARY?

1. Never forget that Mary's role is to bring us to Jesus and to active participation in the life of the Church and the sacraments.
2. Let the texts of the liturgy guide the content of the homilies.
3. Try to see Jesus through Mary's eyes in the Gospel scenes.
4. Emphasize Mary's mission of intercession, but always within the context of her mediation subordinate to Christ's.
5. Respect the role of Mary in popular piety — for example, the Hispanics' devotion to Our Lady of Guadalupe.
6. Honor the approved visions of Mary, certainly those celebrated in liturgies recalling Lourdes and Fatima.
7. Tone down the "signs and wonders" associated with pilgrimage shrines. Focus more on the growth of faith and fervor of prayer that are lasting and fruitful outcomes of such experiences.
8. Avoid fostering the apocalyptic interpretations of Mary's appearances that play on people's fears, incite alarmist feelings, and arouse unwarranted predictions of the end times.
9. Encourage devotion to Mary, especially in the daily recitation of the rosary.
10. Research the history of her feasts, such as the story of the Council of Ephesus that upheld her title of Mother of God, or the background of the liturgy of the Assumption as it prevailed in medieval England, and then in Europe.

in which the judge tells a lawyer, "What you say must not only be true, it must seem true." Yes, truth should be able to speak for itself, but a little help from passionately dedicated defenders will be welcome.

Preaching about Mary in the Liturgy

The frequency of Marian feasts challenges our homiletic creativity to remain faithful to the texts, yet bring fresh insights. St. Ambrose gives us an example of this in his homily on Luke's account of the Visitation:

Notice the contrast and the choice of words. Elizabeth is the first to hear Mary's voice, but John is the first to be aware of grace. She hears with the ears of the body, but he leaps for joy at the meaning of the mystery. She is aware of Mary's presence, but he is aware of the Lord's: a woman aware of a woman's presence, the forerunner aware of the pledge of our salvation. The women speak of the grace they have received, while the children are active in secret, unfolding the mystery of love with the help of their mothers, who prophesy by the spirit of their sons.

— LITURGY OF THE HOURS, VOL. I, PP. 352–3

The feasts of Mary in the liturgy outline her many spiritual privileges and blessings. Immaculately conceived, Mary is the New Eve who consented at the Annunciation to be mother of the Son of God. Remaining ever a virgin, she gave birth to Jesus at Bethlehem . . . heard from Simeon that a sword would pierce her heart due to her connection with Jesus . . . an ache that touched her when she lost her son at the Temple. Upon finding him, she hears him rebuke her for not knowing his calling to be about his Father's interests.

MARIAN ART

What power of inward devotion lies in the images of Mary in the "narrative" art of the Gothic style! They manifest the new humanity of the faith. Such images are an invitation to prayer, because they are permeated by prayer from within. They show us the true image of man as planned by the Creator and renewed by Christ. . . . The images of Christ and the saints are not photographs. Their whole point is to lead us beyond what can be apprehended at the merely material level, to awaken new senses in us, and to teach us a new kind of seeing, which perceives the Invisible in the visible.

— Cardinal Joseph Ratzinger, *The Spirit of the Liturgy*;
Ignatius, San Francisco, 1999, pp. 128 and 133

Christ's public life caused her growing maternal worries, beginning with the negative reaction to his sermon at Nazareth, developing hostility from religious leaders, and finally the overwhelming events of his Passion, death, and burial. Mel Gibson's *Passion of the Christ* views a number of the scenes through Mary's eyes, especially the scene of Mary using towels to soak up his blood after the scourging. Finally, the presence of Mary in the Upper Room, for the nine days of prayer before Pentecost, concludes Scripture's account of her earthly life. The Book of Revelation, chapter 12, hints at her Assumption in the vision of the woman clothed with the sun, crowned with twelve stars, and standing on the moon. The gospels for the Marian feasts in the liturgy recapture most of these aspects of Mary's life and gifts.

There is one small sentence about Mary that attracts my attention: "His mother kept all these things in her heart"(Lk. 2:51). It is usually applied to the troubles she experiences due to her concern for Jesus. I think there is another application that deserves our reflection, namely, her contemplation of her divine Son with love through the days and weeks of the thirty years before he embarks on his public life. I realize we can never know the mystery of their communion in those years — Jesus, somehow quietly revealing his meaning to her, and Mary's faith growth in response. How could one find words to describe the communion of the only two people in history without fallen natures? Small wonder that Scripture calls Jesus the New Adam, and St. Irenaeus named Mary the New Eve.

The philosopher Ludwig Wittgenstein once said, "Whereof I cannot speak, thereof let me be silent." Having shared this interest in the communion of Mary and Jesus with you, I can go no further, and so follow Ludwig's sage counsel.

What are my guidelines for preaching about Mary on her feasts?

Mary, Mother of God, pray for me now and at the hour of my death.

Note to a preacher: "Be good. Be brief. Be gone."

TEN

Preaching Should Be a Prayer, Not a Performance

St. Teresa of Ávila — a Doctor of Prayer (1515–82)

Never be obstinate, especially in unimportant matters. . . . Be kind to others but severe on yourself. . . . Habitually make many acts of love for they set the soul on fire and make it gentle.

— MAXIMS OF ST. TERESA OF ÁVILA

I try to keep reminding myself that preaching should be a prayer, not a performance. Though I need to master the techniques of public speaking and acquire the art of being a public presence, I must never substitute those accomplishments for the spiritual nature of giving a homily. Vanity is always crouching at my feet, subtly inviting me to be full of myself and forgetful of the Christ whom I serve in preaching. The remote preparation for preaching should include a life of prayer. That is why I choose a doctor of prayer, St. Teresa of Ávila, as a guardian angel and the vital guide for this dimension of preaching.

In her youth, Teresa entered the Carmelite convent of the Incarnation of Ávila and remained there for twenty-seven years. She found a congenial and easygoing community, good-spirited but not consumed with the spiritual fervor one might expect in such a community. If anything, this community was like a genteel hotel for the unmarried, upper-class women of Ávila. They did not observe the rules for cloister. They entertained guests in their rooms and treated the visiting areas as though they were hotel lobbies. They thought nothing of leaving the convent for weekends and vacations with relatives and friends.

A personable extrovert, Teresa enjoyed life at the convent — she liked to laugh, dance, and sing — and fell in with their cheerful, casual ways. But soon enough, she began to differ from them in a mounting suspicion that this was not what convent life should be about; she had always felt an attraction to prayer and penance and practiced them regularly. So, through trial and error, with little help from spiritual directors, she happened upon ways to deeper prayer and contemplation. Only after these discoveries did she meet spiritual guides such as Francis Borgia and Peter Alcantara, who understood her and helped her advance in prayer.

At the age of forty-eight, she left her convent and founded a reformed order of Carmelites, the Discalced nuns. She was advised to write an autobiography and an account of her spiritual experiences. Both of these books have become spiritual classics, especially *Interior Castle*.

What does she have to say to us homilists about our prayer life?

(1)

> Pray as you can, for prayer does not consist of thinking a great deal, but of loving a great deal. . . . God can lead to the heights of contemplation one who uses no other words than those of the Lord's Prayer . . . The one absolute rule is that you must never, for any reason, neglect to pray.
> — *INTERIOR CASTLE* IV, I.7; *WAY* XXV, 1; *COUNSELS* 184, 188

(2) Madre Teresa emphasized living the Christian life and the importance of growth in Christian virtues as the necessary pre-requisites "for those who aim to follow the way of prayer — so necessary that, even if one isn't much of a contemplative, they will help one forward greatly in the service of the Lord, and it isn't possible to be much of a contemplative without them. The first is love for one another; the second is (emotional) detachment from all created things; the third is true humility" (*Way* iv, 3–4). The quality of your life and the quality of your prayer exercise a mutual effect on each other.

(3) Finally, St. Teresa urges us to think constantly of the humanity of Jesus, who dwells in us as a friend:

> Many, many times I have perceived this through experience. . . . Let us consider the glorious St. Paul. It seems that no other name fell from his lips than that of Jesus, because the name of Jesus was fixed and embedded in his heart. . . . Let us strive to keep this always before our eyes and to rouse ourselves to love him. For if at some

time the Lord should grant us the grace of impressing his love on our hearts, all will become easy for us and we shall accomplish great things quickly and without effort.

— LITURGY OF THE HOURS, VOL. IV, PP. 1483–4

THE WAY OF PRAYER

We must maintain great stillness of mind, even in the midst of our struggles. . . . A tranquil sea allows the fisherman to gaze right into its depths. No fish can hide there and escape his sight. The stormy sea, however, becomes murky when it is agitated by the winds. The very depths that it revealed in its placidness, the sea now hides. The skills of the fisherman are useless. . . . So by every means, especially by peace of soul, we must try to provide the Holy Spirit a resting place. Then we will have the light of knowledge shining within us at all times. . . . When our mind is strong and free of all anxiety, it is able to taste the riches of divine consolation.

— Bishop Diadochus, Liturgy of the Hours,
Vol. III, pp. 154–5

Prayerful Homilies

When we strive to live the Christian life, practice Christian virtues, and have an active prayer life, we will have a prayerful attitude when we preach. We will also spontaneously find opportunities to promote prayer in our homilies. The Gospels record that Jesus prayed many times, both in public and alone all night on a mountain. This so impressed his apostles that they asked him to teach them to pray. As you know, he taught them the Our Father in response to their request. So deep is this prayer that the Church's greatest homilists have written commentaries on it. The Liturgy of the Hours contains one of St. Augustine's meditations on the Our Father, as well as a commentary on it by St. Cyprian of Carthage.

I think people really appreciate occasional advice on how to pray better. Here are seven tips on weaving into our homilies helps on prayer for our people.

1. At least once a month, show how your message on the Word of God leads people to the praise of God in the Eucharist and deeper union with Christ in Communion. The gospel of the cure of the Roman centurion's servant is an ideal time to do this, especially noting his words that he is not worthy to have Jesus enter his home. These words of a pagan soldier are used in every Mass before Communion.

2. The prayers for healing that occur in many Gospels are a good time to speak about the power of prayer. The poet Tennyson says it well: "More things are wrought by prayer than this world dreams of. Wherefore, let thy voice rise like a fountain for me day and night."

3. In chapter 9, I recommended that on feasts of Mary, or other times when Mary is mentioned in the Gospel, there is an opening to encourage people to pray the rosary and to show them how to do it more effectively. Recommend small prayer pamphlets that provide pictures, brief meditations, a virtue to practice, and an intention to make to go with each mystery. This focuses their attention to the mysteries.

4. Following the guidance of St. Teresa of Ávila already mentioned, you could show people the link between Christian witness and prayer, how one reinforces the other. As Teresa might put it, "It's hard to be good at prayer if you are not trying to be a good Christian."

An old woman tells the story of how she was in a hospital and full of pain. She did not have the courage to take the tests that would tell her what was wrong. One morning, a member of her parish visited her and told her that a group of her friends was forming a prayer circle for her. They planned to spend a whole night praying for her. That night she slept like a child and, in the morning, was strong enough to take the needed tests.

5. Mini-lessons on meditation are always desirable and can be easily inserted in almost any homily on the Gospel, as many scenes they depict are visually memorable. People can mentally enter into the scene, understand the characters, and grasp their relation to Jesus. St. Ignatius directs his beginners to do this and actually never give up the practice, no matter how advanced they might be in prayer. St. Teresa says the same.

6. While formal prayers such as the Hail Mary and the Our Father are the staples of everybody's piety, people need training in heart prayer, or talking to God in a simple and personal manner. Homilists need to help them acquire this habit. You can do this by modeling it from your own life, sharing a personal prayer you recently addressed to God, or borrowing a passage from the *Confessions of St. Augustine*, which is filled with this kind of prayer. This is not telling God something he doesn't know; it is reciting what gifts from God we need to be aware of.

7. Lastly, help them to find the patience to practice "Listening Prayer." Read again the passage on tranquility in prayer from Bishop Diadochus on p. 69. Everyone can calm down, find ways to be quiet, so that the soul can hear what God wants to communicate to them. The current popularity of "Centering Prayer" reflects both the need of, and the opportunity to teach and explain, this sort of prayer.

These seven tips can be seamlessly introduced into your homilies, once you realize the value of teaching your people to pray and you become aware of the hunger they have. They want to pray better, but many of them need explicit encouragement and training in how to do it. I have outlined a pattern of praying in which there is an essential unity in the various aspects of prayer, a union of love with God. Of all the impacts of our homilies, this can be one of the greatest. "O Homilist, teach us to pray!"

How have I been teaching my people to pray?

Jesus, teach me to pray.

Humor is the beginning of faith, and laughter is the beginning of prayer.

— Reinhold Niebuhr

ELEVEN

Humor in Homilies?

St. Philip Neri (1515–1595):
God's clown became the Apostle of Rome

Philip Neri worried a lot about his image, but maybe not in the way you might think. He was determined people would *not* mistake him for a saint, and so adopted eccentricities designed to make people think he was slightly foolish. A clown by nature, he often strolled through Rome wearing his clothes inside out, along with floppy white shoes, to amuse those who stared at him. He dispelled the idea that saints should be solemn. The child in him found mischievous ways to disarm people, such as occasionally shaving only half his beard or strutting around with a large blue cushion perched on his head.

When pompous clergy came to dine with him, Philip entertained them by bringing out a monkey wearing a miniature bishop's miter and carrying a gun. Responding to an ascetic impulse, a disciple of Philip asked permission to wear a hair shirt. Philip agreed, "Yes, you may have your hair shirt, but you must wear it outside your coat and not next to your skin." The man felt embarrassed. Philip judged correctly that an itch to one's ego was the greater mortification than bodily discomfort.

Philip was an enthusiastic enemy of vanity. Listening to a sermon by one of his newly ordained priests, he sensed the young man was too full of his self-importance. Philip deflated that attitude by ordering the man to give the same sermon on the following six Sundays. By the last Sunday, the people were saying, "Here comes the one-sermon priest."

Born in Florence, Philip went to Rome to study philosophy and theology. At the completion of his studies, he did not present himself for ordination. Rather, he embarked on a thirteen-year career as a lay minister in Rome. At that time, Luther's Reformation was in full swing. Rome was a city of lazy priests, corrupt officials, and a paganized laity. The Council of Trent that would spur the Counter-Reformation was only just beginning. Philip Neri would become the spiritual architect for the reform of the city of Rome. It all began slowly and simply enough. He felt an intense inner drive to contemplative prayer to which he devoted substantial time each day. Over the years, his prayer acquired a mystical depth, at times even inducing trances. He later said that his clowning around helped him retain his self-possession at Eucharist and in his active ministry.

He engaged in traditional works for the poor and built a hospital for cash-poor pilgrims. After thirteen years, he became a priest. He obtained a building where he sponsored afternoon seminars on the Bible, Church history, the spiritual life, and the lives of the saints. There were normally four sessions of speeches and discussions, interspersed with prayer and music. These sessions were held in what he called an Oratory, or Prayer Room. Philip invited great composers such as Palestrina to write music to fit Scripture dialogues he had composed. These dramatic choral music works were soon called "oratorios" — later developed further by Bach and Handel.

He also spent many hours hearing confessions. As disciples gathered around him, he formed some of them into a new religious community, the Oratorians. Among them were the outstanding Church historian, Caesar Baronius, and, much later on, one of Christianity's greatest preachers — Cardinal John Henry Newman.

Though Philip liked to clown around, he was dead serious when it came to training laity and clergy alike in prayer, Scripture, ecclesiastical history, theology, and classical music. The Council of Trent would catch up with him by ordering the creation of seminaries for a thorough formation and education of future priests.

Humor's Treacherous Waters

I used the quirky humor of Philip Neri not as an example to be imitated, but to free up a homilist to use humor when it is appropriate. Most of us know that literally adopting some of the clownish ways of Philip Neri will probably never work — and most likely will be counterproductive, leading our people to write to the bishop suggesting a straitjacket for "poor Father." In fact we ought not try to be someone else in any case, whether in humor or in feats of solemnity. Each one of us is a unique

HOW TO USE HUMOR PROPERLY IN A HOMILY

1. Have a purpose.

Pastor John Ortberg believes that because "the ultimate goal of preaching is to have Christ formed in people," humor must always be the servant of the message. If humor does nothing to forward that purpose, then the preacher should jettison it from the sermon.

2. Observe daily life.

Humor flowing from life experiences always trumps jokes with punch lines. Jokes are what comedian Ken Davis calls high-risk humor. If a joke dies, everyone knows it, and the point may die with it. When a personal story does not elicit the laugh you thought it would, it still maintains the power to illustrate the point. That's why Davis calls this low-risk humor and suggests this is where someone trying to learn to be more humorous should begin. So avoid joke books and pay more attention to what is going on around you.

3. Keep the surprise.

Saying "Let me tell you something funny" is disastrous. It's harder to surprise people. For some, an automatic resistance kicks in. They cross their arms and think, *I'll be the judge of that.*

4. Credit sources.

Nothing dampens the effectiveness of humor more surely or our credibility more quickly than presenting someone else's humor or someone else's experience as our own.

> — *Christianity Today.Com*: John Beukema,
> excerpted from *Preaching Today.Com*,
> Autumn 2004

In 1964, Robert Short wrote a book, *The Gospel According to Peanuts*, using Charles Schulz's comic strips as illustrations of religious messages. He followed it in 1968 with a second work, *The Parables of Peanuts*. Here is the dialogue from one of the strips:

> Lucy: I want to talk to you, Charlie Brown. As your sister's consulting psychiatrist, I must put the blame for her fears on you.
>
> Charlie: (startled and defensive) On me?
>
> Lucy: Each generation must be able to blame the previous generations for its problems. (walking away) It doesn't solve anything, but it makes us all feel better.
>
> — Robert L. Short, HarperSanFrancisco, pp. 55–56

Over the years many a homilist (including me) has mined the *Peanuts* comic strips to illustrate Gospel truths presented in a wise and humorous way.

homilist created especially by God for the special purpose he has for us in the role of homilist. Aping others wastes time and robs the Church of the benefit it could receive from the spiritual gifts God has given each of us to use in our ministry.

Having said this, it is equally important to caution those who have no native sense of humor from trying to be funny. To a person with a sense of humor, "all the world's a stage" from which one garners a constant treasury of laughs. To a person without humor — whatever the mysterious reason for this — the world may look witty, and he can get a laugh out of it, but he lacks the funny bone to translate it into an amusing remark. In this case, he wisely uses other rhetorical gifts to create a persuasive homily. If he lamely tries to use a canned joke, the outcome is not just a groaner, but a gasp.

On the other hand, most homilists have a reserve of humor that can be employed in modest amounts. Once in a while, a funny story or a joke serves as an icebreaker for a homily. It will be more effective if it actually relates to the ideas in the homily. A skillful speaker will make connections between humor and substance. He will use this method sparingly, so that he is not trapped by setting up comic expectations which are hard to maintain unless you have a team of writers who supply you with a steady diet of one-liners. A congregation is more likely to be tolerant of even "lame" humor once they have gotten to know the preacher and his strengths and weaknesses, terms of endearment, and forgivable follies.

Also, because humor is equated with entertainment in our culture, it's prudent to use it sparingly in homilies. Great humorists are few and far between. A Mark Twain and a Will Rogers are exceptions. They made humor an art form and even a kind of folk wisdom veering into philosophy, but a homilist who comes across as a comedian may soon be dismissed as a lightweight who has little of depth to communicate. Many people resist the "entertainment model" when it intrudes into the sanctuary; they've become wary of our culture that wants to amuse us to death. So when it comes to humor and the homily, "less is more."

A gentle touch of humor now and then spreads warmth; too much can backfire. Therefore, homilists, tread lightly in this area.

How do I manage to insert humor into my homilies? Or do I?

Dear God, give me a sense of humor.

Years ago, in County Galway, Ireland, a newly ordained priest decided that he would devote his first homily to the subject of Christian marriage, since the Gospel passage for that Sunday was the Marriage feast at Cana.

After Mass, two elderly ladies were discussing his homily. Bridget said, "Ah, didn't that fine young priest give a grand sermon today?" Nora replied, "Indeed, he did. I wish I knew as little about marriage as he does."

TWELVE

Wedding Homilies

St. Elizabeth Ann Bayley Seton

By the law of the Church that I love so much, I could never take an obligation that interfered with my duties to my children.

— ELIZABETH SETON, LETTER TO A FRIEND

The first American Roman Catholic saint was born a Protestant.

Elizabeth Ann Bayley came from old New York money and the blessings of the Episcopal Church. At age sixteen, she fell in love with William Magee Seton, a rich businessman. Three years later, they were married at New York's fashionable Trinity Church, whose pastor, the formidable Reverend Henry Hobart, soon became her spiritual director. He sought to deepen her commitment to Christianity through his evangelical view of how a good Episcopalian should live. Elizabeth sought more than a humanitarian type of religion and welcomed Hobart's efforts to deepen her faith.

Mrs. Seton gave birth to three girls and two boys. Then, in the ninth year of her marriage, a series of woes began to afflict her family. Her husband's business collapsed and his health along with it. An Italian business acquaintance and longtime friend of the Setons, Antonio Fillichi, invited William, Elizabeth, and their oldest daughter, Anna, to come to live with his family in Leghorn, Italy. He believed a change of pace and place, as well as a lengthy rest, would lead to William's recovery of health and a new start in life. They accepted his offer.

Unfortunately, William died six weeks after their arrival in Italy. The Fillichis surrounded Elizabeth and Anna with love and support during their mourning period. Their affection and devout Catholicism touched Elizabeth deeply. By the time she was embarking for the United States six months later, she was well on her way to becoming a Catholic. Antonio accompanied the widow and her daughter back to the States, where a joyful restoration of the family occurred.

Elizabeth then pondered her options. Should she look for a new husband? How was she going to rebuild her life and make a living and support her five children? The matter was complicated by her growing desire to become a Catholic. Practically speaking, this would not be a good move. It would anger her relatives and friends and eliminate the contacts she needed for survival. This was not an ecumenical age. The passions that divided Protestants and Catholics in Europe were carried with them across the Atlantic into America; there, the Catholic community was small and without influence. The Protestant majority constituted the ruling class.

Elizabeth struggled with these dilemmas for a year, at the end of which she joined the Catholic Church on March 4, 1805. Father Matthew O'Brien, pastor of St. Peter's Church on Barclay Street, welcomed her "home."

She had long nourished a love for teaching and tried several times to start a small school, but failed. Then, she was invited to open a Catholic school in Baltimore. It provided free education for the poor, while charging tuition from those who could afford it. Her success with Catholic education, linked with her founding an American version of the Sisters of Charity, led to her being considered the foundress of the Catholic school system in the United States.

Her busy life included her constant care for her own children. Her daughters were raised in the religious community until adulthood, but her two boys were enrolled at Georgetown. Like most mothers, she worried about her boys. She wanted William to be a banker. Instead, he chose to be a seaman. She sent him a steady stream of maternal letters:

> Now, my love, I must hope you are safe in your berth. You must fill a station and take a part in our life of trial, and all your mother can beg is that you keep well with your pilot and as says Robert Burns, "the correspondence fixed with heaven will be your noble anchor."

Her son eventually settled down, married, and sired some sons, one of whom became an archbishop. She lived a life of heroic virtue, both as a married woman and mother and as a religious. The Church canonized her in 1976.

God is the author of marriage. In God's plan marriage has two goals: (1) Unitive Love in which the spouses pledge everlasting love and fidelity to one another; (2) Procreative Love in which the spouses are open to the possibility of children whom they will beget, nurture and raise.

The Bible's teaching about marriage begins with the Lord's creation of man and woman who become two in one flesh and ends with a vision of the marriage feast of the Lamb. Scripture constantly speaks of marriage, its "mystery," its history, its problems and its renewal in the covenant Jesus made with the Church.

God created marriage. It is not a purely human institution, despite the changes it has experienced in different cultures and social situations. We should be more aware of the common and permanent features of marriage. All cultures sense the greatness of marriage, even if not with the same perceptiveness. Most of the world's peoples believe that a healthy marriage is important for a wholesome society and the human and Christian good of the individual.

Marital love should be an image of the absolute and unfailing love God has for every human being. Scripture teaches that man and woman were created for one another. "It is not good that the man should be alone." (Gen. 2:18) The woman is his counterpart and his equal. Jesus repeated the teaching of Genesis when he declared that marriage ought to be an unbreakable union, for man and woman are no longer two, but one flesh. (Cf. Mt. 19:6)

— Fr. Alfred McBride, *College Catechism*, OSV, p. 173

Composing Your Wedding Homily

I selected the story of St. Elizabeth Ann Seton to highlight the fact that married people can be canonized saints. At least eleven of the apostles (with the traditional exception of St. John)were married and are celebrated as saints in the liturgy. The same is true of most of the popes in the first 200 years of the Church, virtually all of whom were martyred.

But, aside from Christ's cure of Peter's mother-in-law, we have no record of the apostle's marital and family life, nor of any of the martyred and married papal saints of the early centuries.

In the second millennium of Christianity, few married people, other than some kings and queens and St. Thomas More, were canonized. Hence the special importance of St. Elizabeth Ann Seton. I certainly do not imply that her example should be inserted regularly in wedding homilies, but a preacher can certainly approach the homily from the assurance that married people do have God's call to holiness and that some have been canonized.

I think that marriage preparation and the wedding homily should be thought of as a continuum. The best advice on this comes from Msgr. Joseph Champlin, who has pioneered this approach in his excellent booklet, *Together For Life*. The relationship built up between the homilist and the couple being prepared for the wedding is a rich source for the homily. It is an evangelizing time in which the couple can be drawn once again to renew their faith in Jesus Christ, about whom we proclaim in the Mass, "By your cross and resurrection, you have set us free. You are the Savior of the world."

I also realize that my readers range from veteran pastors and deacons to freshly-minted ones. My few "rules" are merely generally accepted guides that can be adapted by anyone. Wedding situations are as variable as the ethnic enclaves, settings — ranging from villages to large cities — and the economic and educational status of the couple. I hope these universals fit most situations.

Five Easy Rules for Wedding Homilies

1. At beginning of Mass, say some reassuring words to the couple. Relax them. Calm them down and introduce the faith aspect of the sacrament. Then, to the whole assembly, welcome the parents and families and friends of the bride and groom. These days, the guests will include people of other faiths or persuasions. A Christian welcome is best, one in which our common humanity is evident.

2. Begin your homily by speaking directly to the couple, such as: "John and Mary, this will be one of the happiest days of your

life. Treasure each moment of this experience . . ." Create intimacy between yourself and the couple and dispel any nervousness they may be feeling. By beginning with a personal touch, you indirectly involve the congregation, whom you proceed to address along with the couple.

3. Tell a brief story. If you were involved with the couple in their marriage preparation, you could listen for little human stories from them that mean a lot to them. Use one of these stories, if it seems appropriate and relate it to your message. You could also use stories from older couples who have celebrated their silver or golden wedding anniversaries, wisdom stories to encourage the bride and groom.

4. The remainder of your message should be related to the readings or other liturgical texts and be as encouraging as possible. Don't dwell on the sad state of marriage today, the rising divorce rate, the declining birth rate, or the materialism of our society. There are other times for that. Be positive, upbeat, and hope-filled.

5. As the bride and groom make their vows, it's often a nice touch to invite married couples in the assembly to renew their own vows quietly as well.

What structure do I use in my wedding homilies?

Dear God, author of marriage, make my wedding homilies better.

It is said that Elizabeth Seton found great comfort in identifying with the will of God. God's will and God's love were one and the same to her. From her family, her religion, and her God, she absorbed the supreme lesson of Love. It's the best lesson any saint can teach married people.

THIRTEEN

Funeral Homilies

St. Paul the Apostle

O death, where is thy sting? O grave, where is thy victory? (KJV)

I imagine some think it odd that I would pick St. Paul as a source for funeral homilies, but few saints of Christian history have written more compellingly about death and resurrection than Paul. Not only did he endure a cruel martyr's death, he faced constant lethal threats to his life throughout his missionary exploits. He summarized them in a scary list of physical tortures that would leave many others dead before the sequence was completed:

> Are they servants of Christ? I am a better one — I am talking like a madman — with far greater labors, far more imprisonments, with countless beatings, and often near death. . . . Three times I have been beaten with rods, once I was stoned. Three times I have been shipwrecked; a night and a day I have been adrift at sea; on frequent journeys, in danger from rivers, danger from robbers, danger from my own people, danger from Gentiles, danger in the city, danger in the wilderness, danger at sea, danger from false brethren; in toil and hardship, through many a sleepless night, in hunger and thirst, often without food, in cold and exposure. . . . Who is weak and I am not weak?. . . If I must boast, I will boast of the things that show my weakness. The God and Father of our Lord Jesus Christ, he who is blessed forever, knows that I do not lie.
>
> — 2 COR. 11: 23–31

The shadow of death besieged Paul through most of his apostolate. His sufferings are a list of near-death experiences that pursued him for over thirty years as a missionary. He was no stranger to the possibility of death. To those of you who saw the scourging scene in Mel Gibson's *The Passion of the Christ*, you could imagine Paul's being scourged — though perhaps not with as many lashes as in the film — but even a third of such beatings is horrendous, and the recovery must have been lengthy and enervating.

Not only did Paul have real-time encounters with death-dealing attacks, he also wrote about the death of Christ and its meaning. In the first two chapters of his first letter to the Corinthians, Paul dwelt on the centrality of the death of Christ in his preaching. Repeatedly he contrasted the wisdom of this world with the wisdom of the Cross. Worldly wisdom does not offer salvation, but the death of Jesus is the very source of salvation. In his letter to the Romans (Rom. 6:3–6), he explained that the meaning of Baptism is related to dying with Christ as we descend into the baptismal waters so that our sins may be forgiven, and to rising with him to new life as we ascend from the waters. Once you start combing Paul's writings, you become aware of his recurring references to the Passion as an essential feature of our salvation.

When he speaks of faith as necessary for our redemption, he links it with faith in Christ, who died and rose to save us. This brings us to his other teaching about death as the door to the resurrection of our bodies with Christ. The Easter narratives in the Gospels announce Christ's bodily resurrection; Paul's sermon on the resurrection, in chapter 15 of his first letter to the Corinthians, is the best scriptural commentary on the link between Christ's bodily resurrection and ours. No other significant section of Scripture proclaims our bodily resurrection so forcefully.

Paul begins with a stirring act of faith in Christ's resurrection, bolstered by the testimony of apostolic witnesses and 500 others. Then, he argues that if Jesus had not risen, our faith would be in vain, and the possibility of our resurrection is unthinkable. But Jesus did rise and the last enemy, namely death, shall be overcome by all. Death is not the end. Our life is changed; it does not pass away into nothingness. Paul concludes with his sonorous word picture, "The trumpet will sound, and the dead shall be raised imperishable, and we shall be changed" (1 Cor. 15:52). Paul had no illusions about physical death that he faced so often. He lifted that experience into his vision of the paschal mystery by which Jesus accomplishes his salvation of our souls and bodies.

Funerals, like weddings, occur often enough so that the homilist needs to avoid the dullness of "routine" in his approach. He will be effective in proportion to his pastoral sensitivity to the mourners and his skill as a liturgical celebrant.

HOW TO FIND STORIES FOR A FUNERAL HOMILY

1. The best way is to be alert for stories at the wake before the funeral. Also look for stories from your hospital or home visits to the dying person.
2. If one or both of your parents — or a sibling — has died, are there stories related to their deaths that you would like to tell?
3. If you have lost a sister or brother, you may find a story about this that could be told.
4. If you have been a hospice visitor, you may have stories of people who showed inspiring faith as they neared the end.
5. Do you have friends who have passed away whose final days remind you of incidents you could share?
6. Was there a priest or religious, now deceased, whose courage in dealing with death touched you?
7. Think of public figures who have died, such as Blessed Teresa of Calcutta and Pope John Paul II. Were there stories surrounding their deaths and funerals that you might use?
8. Is there a death scene in a film you have seen or a book you have read that would be appropriate for your homily?

Compassion for the mourners is itself a living homily. Conducting the service with dignity and reverence is an antidote to the weight of repetition. The homily is part of a larger ministry that includes the anointing of the sick, the visits to the ill, the preparation for the funeral with the bereaved, and the wake service. The varieties of death, from that of the elderly to the death of a child, from the tragic death of a young parent to the loss of a widely respect public figure, from the passing of a controversial person to someone revered as a saint — all these passages challenge the homilist in different ways.

Following, I list some rules about the service that provide a comfort structure for the homilist. Even in the homily itself, there is a structure of material that should be the evangelical core of what is preached. Generally this means:

1. The Christian meaning of suffering and death is found in the passion, death, and resurrection of Christ
2. First of all, this means that life is changed, not taken away. The soul of the person lives on. We should continue to pray for the deceased, that he or she be taken into eternal life with God.
3. Secondly, the paschal mystery means that the person's body will rise again at the Last Judgment.

Creativity in expressing these home truths is a daunting task for a homilist who has been in a parish for many years and presided over many funerals. Often, the same people appear at many funerals. Perhaps my "home truths" can be spread out, one or another at different funerals. The variety of scriptural readings — including the psalms — can help in this regard.

These days, people in the congregation can often be inactive Catholics, people of other faiths, or people with no faith at all. A gentle outreach, through clear and loving presentation of the basics of the Catholic beliefs about death and the future life, are genuine gifts for such participants. It is not a time for proselytizing. It is an occasion for celebrating and witnessing Christian death and resurrection.

Rules for Funeral Homilies

1. Begin with words of sympathy for relatives and friends. Be warm, personal, and consoling.
2. Next, briefly refer to the paschal candle that symbolizes the presence of the risen Christ, who leads our friend to the Kingdom. Explain the white pall, or robe, over the casket that recalls the baptismal robe received by our beloved (name), who has completed the earthly journey. The liturgical prayers say this, of course, but it seems to help by expressing these truths in a more spontaneous way.
3. In your homily, it usually is best to address your opening words to the mourning family, and then extend your comments to the whole congregation. It's also important to balance homily and eulogy, giving preference to the homily. In some places, the deceased is prematurely "canonized" at the funeral. Of course,

good things should be said, and virtues upheld — but the attention should be on Christ and his saving graces.

It is certainly fitting to tell a brief story about the deceased. If you were at the deceased's bedside at the hospital, hospice, or home — or were at the wake service — you should be alert to personal stories about him/her that you can bring to this homily (see sidebar).

4. An excellent summary of the Church's teaching on death and future life is the preface for the Mass of Christian Burial. Relate the homily to messages from liturgical readings or other liturgical texts. If it is a child's funeral, speak of Christ's special love for children and of heaven. Always give hope in eternal life. If baby was not baptized, recall the teaching of the *Catechism*: "God has bound salvation to the sacraments, but he himself is not bound to sacraments" (1257). Also #1261, where the *Catechism* says, "Entrust them to the mercy of God who desires that all should be saved; and Jesus' tenderness to children . . . that allows us to hope that there is a way of salvation for children who have died without baptism."

5. If possible, close with a memorable saying, such as "The only things we take with us to the next world are what we have given away," or something else appropriate to the situation. [*NB*: If possible, have guest eulogies at the wake service. Or, if a eulogy is given after Communion, do whatever you can to keep it short.]

How do I remain creative in my funeral homilies?

Merciful Jesus, help me to be compassionate at funerals.

Therefore, my beloved brethren, be steadfast, immovable, always abounding in the work of the Lord, knowing that in the Lord your labor is not in vain.

— 1 Cor. 15:58

FOURTEEN

Some Preaching Lessons from Cardinal Newman

Homilies on saints, his pulpit presence, his skill in writing sermons and reading them effectively

Newman's Homiletic Approach to Saints

John Henry Newman was supposed to have said, "I could never be named a saint. I've written a novel!" Nonetheless, he was an ardent student of the spiritual life and nurtured his strong attraction to holiness. During his Anglican years Newman often preached about saints, though not about the theory of sanctity. Throughout his fifteen years at St. Mary's University Church in Oxford, Newman preached not only on Sundays but also on feasts of saints. These talks may be found in his *Parochial and Plain Sermons* (happily reprinted in one volume by St. Ignatius Press).

He never spoke about the saints as finished products, more like sinners making progress in grace. Newman realized that many lives of the saints focused on the heroic virtues of saintly people, but ignored the process by which the saint was brought to the fullness of holiness. Other than the Blessed Mother, saints were born with fallen natures. They needed conversion from sin to grace. The drama of their conversion was often overlooked. Their moment of truth was bypassed. Newman would have none of this. He had an uncanny eye for the master flaw of a given saint and showed how God's grace used that "thorn in the flesh" to guide the person to growth in virtue.

It is in these sermons that he often illustrated the power of prayer, which he called a "robe of light." Here, we may uncover his spiritual insights. He does not arrive in that fabled pulpit still to be seen and venerated as the controversial theologian. He came as a pastor resolute on struggling for the souls of his congregation. However, we must not imagine him as a fire-breathing homilist. Newman distrusted emotion not restrained by authority and reason.

Newman's Pulpit Presence

Those who heard him tell us that he gave his hour-long sermons with no dramatics. He spoke in a plain high pitched voice with barely any inflections. He hands rested on the lectern — no emphatic use of gestures. All the observers remark that at times he would pause briefly, and in that silence allow them to move with him to his conclusions. What kept their attention was the interior energy that flowed from his presence. It is what we would call today the witness of his holiness, his own internal life with God.

Hushed congregations of Oxford students, professors, and university workers packed St. Mary's for years to listen to Newman describe the story of their souls. He knew how to surface their moral challenges and how they were dealing with them. He identified their difficulties with faith, reminding them that a thousand difficulties do not make one doubt. He was uncompromising in bringing them face-to-face with the grandeur of the mysteries of Christ. There was very little that was obviously topical about his talks. No fads or fashions of the day to any extent. Only the rich and powerful words of Scripture, and the doctrines of the ancient Church, coupled with an extraordinary ability to narrate the history of the souls who sat before him.

Newman understood that the life of the Spirit flowed from years of familiarity with the Scriptures. His hypnotic power came from a unity within his person, for he believed that the heart makes the theologian as much as the mind — "The God of my theology is the God to whom I pray." As an Oratorian, Newman was devoted to St. Philip Neri, the founder of that congregation. From this saint, Newman adopted principles such as: Do what God intended me to do. Live constantly in the presence of God. Remain obedient to the moral life. Gentility, knowledge, and science never healed the wounded heart. Only Jesus Christ can really do that.

Newman's Move to Catholicism

When Newman decided to leave Oxford University and reflect on the next stage of his spiritual journey, he retired to Littlemore, three miles away. With some disciples, he transformed a former stable into something like a small monastery, arranged around a garden. The little community lived a modified monastic life. Newman lived there four years, at the conclusion of which he entered the Catholic Church.

Today, the Sisters of the Work have taken over the property and have made it a Newman Shrine and a place for research. His library is now a museum. Bookcases contain Newman's collected works, as well as numerous books about him. Pictures of him and his family line the walls. Prominently placed is Newman's desk, where he wrote his theological masterpiece, *The Development of Christian Doctrine*. The desk looks like a podium, with the writing part on a slant, since Newman wrote this text standing up. It was his last book as an Anglican.

At its completion, Newman was visited by the Passionist priest, Dominic Barbieri (now a Blessed), who welcomed him into the Church. The following morning, Fr. Barbieri laid the writing desk flat and offered Mass on the very place where Newman's latest book had been written. Newman received his First Communion by a space that radiated his remarkable insight into centuries of growth of developing understanding of Christian doctrine. His own faith had developed much as he described the process of the Church's faith. In his diary, Newman wrote, "At last all my prayers have been answered."

To Read or Not to Read . . . a Homily?

Newman wrote each of his sermons as though they were literary accomplishments. He was blessed with an artistic temperament that lent

WHAT MAKES A GREAT SERMON?

Often the preacher's personality contributes, and by all accounts the very presence of John Henry Newman enhanced the spell of his words. Matthew Arnold wrote these famous words about him:

> Who could resist the charm of that spiritual apparition, gliding in the dim afternoon light through the aisle of St. Mary's, rising into the pulpit, and then in the most entrancing of voices, breaking the silence with words and thoughts which were religious music — subtle, sweet, mournful?

his sermons their literary force. They also happened to be partly a diary of his soul in quest of God as well as his desire to enter into the history of the souls of his listeners. With an Augustinian flair for noting his own spiritual struggles, he developed an acute awareness of the spiritual adventures of his listeners.

Great nineteenth-century preachers typically wrote their sermons and read them from the pulpit, usually in a dramatic voice with accompanying gestures. Newman followed suit, except that he avoided theatricality, allowing instead the power of his prose and the energy of his soul to be the servant of the Holy Spirit, to whom he entrusted his words. Hence the written sermons had additional value beyond their use in the liturgy.

Should we write out our homilies? I think this would benefit our effort to be coherent in our preaching, more careful in sticking to one point, and more conscious of the links between the stages of our talks. Cicero wrote, "He who would learn how to speak publicly should first learn how to write [his talks]." Writing down your thoughts shows you how "transparent" your expression is of what you think. The printed page is a monitor of your thought and an excellent teacher of how to be simple, clear, and direct.

Should we do this all the time? Probably not. Sometimes? Yes.

One of the problems of a written homily is that it "freezes" your thinking to that of the time you wrote it. It also tempts some to memorize their homilies, but this can lead to disaster, as most preachers don't have great memories!

I recommend the following three steps:

1. Outline the written text. Then, tear up your text or mail it to yourself so you won't retreat to it.
2. Redo your outline to a shorter one. Shred the longer one.
3. Finally, reduce the second outline to a few key words and preach from them. This will enable you to preach ideas and heartfelt thoughts.

Should we read a written homily? Some homilists are effective in doing this; most are not. Many who read their homilies do so in a dead tone, fail to look at their listeners, and allow no pauses to help their audience keep pace with the thoughts expressed. If you insist on reading your homily, I suggest the following:

- Read it out loud to yourself. You should write the material to be read to be heard. Have someone videotape you and then watch the tape.
- Get two listeners and read it out loud to them. Invite their comments and be open to them.
- Then ask each listener to read your homily to you. This holds up a mirror to your words. It will be a salutary experience.

Overall, using very brief outlines seems to be the best solution and one that I've noticed is generally employed by effective preachers. Obviously, there are formal occasions, such as jubilee events, that call for a written and read homily. In the long run, though, what you can best learn from Newman the preacher was his extraordinary devotion to the preaching ministry. He was a gifted preacher and understood its value for the Church. His commitment to holiness was the condition for the effectiveness of his homilies. These ideals are eminently worth imitating.

What kind of a person am I? How does it help my preaching?

Holy Spirit, lead me along the path to holiness.

Cardinal Newman learned early in his life the need to trust in God if he would make progress in sanctity. In this stanza of a familiar hymn, he expresses that trust in God to "take charge."

Lead, kindly Light, amid the encircling gloom.
   Lead Thou me on.
The night is dark and I am far from home. Lead Thou me on.
Keep Thou my feet, I do not ask to see
the distant shore — one step enough for me.

FIFTEEN

Children's Homilies

St. Thérèse of Lisieux (1873–1897):
her "little way" of spiritual childhood

Much is made of the term "little" in the life of Thérèse of Lisieux —
Little Thérèse or the Little Way. Actually, the "little" woman was
a giant.

To her, "little" never meant small, diminutively sweet, or limp. It
actually referred to her simplicity, a trait found in geniuses — religious,
scientific, or otherwise. Her "little" is more akin to the "small is beautiful" and "less is more" tastes of our day. This is one reason she has cap-
tivated intellectuals while attracting mass appeal at the same time.
Because Thérèse Martin never lost her "inner child" and used its inno-
cence and wonder as a guiding light for her spirituality, it seems to me
she is an ideal presence to guide preachers for children's homilies.

Consistent with the theme of the aura of youth, Sr. Thérèse of the
Child Jesus died at the young age of twenty-four. She left behind a spiritual testament, *The Story of a Soul,* an autobiography that has sold millions of copies. In her book, Thérèse made two promises that have
intrigued and inspired a vast following. Her first promise, "After my
death I will let fall a shower of roses," was received by people who took
her at her word and sought miracles and spiritual favors from her. The
Carmel at Lisieux has documented many thousands of pages of answers
to prayers seeking the intercession of St. Thérèse.

Her second promise was "I will come back to earth to teach others
to love Love." Millions have felt that love and returned it with enthusiasm. This was the secret of her little way of spiritual childhood. In a time
when religious legalism and an emphasis on guilt marked the "fire and
brimstone" sermons of parish missions and spiritual direction, her lessons of love exploded on the scene as a healthy alternative. She recovered for popular piety the truth about divine love as God's principal way

of relating to us. She put new life into Christ's greatest commandments, love of God and love of neighbor.

She took away the exhaustion promoted by the spiritual guides who wore out their clients by pushing them to win God's favor by spiritual gymnastics instead of accepting God's love and passing it on to others. She purposely spoke of the small events of everyday life and made them the stepping stones to God when performed with great love.

For her, it did not matter whether one was rich and powerful, or a brilliant scientist, or a master artist. Remarkably, she understood that even the days of what we would call an "overachiever" were usually filled with hundreds of humdrum acts that probably would never garner a headline. Those small moments in the lives of great people needed love of God and neighbor just as much as did those who passed their days in humbler pursuits.

Thérèse was born in Alençon, France, of Louis Martin, a watch-maker, and his wife, Zelie. Thérèse's mother died when she was five, so she was raised by her older sisters and an aunt. Outwardly, she led the cozy, comfortable middle-class life of her times — albeit in a very devout family. Her father was a man of deep faith, and her two older sisters entered the Carmel at Lisieux. So it wasn't surprising when, early on, Thérèse demonstrated a precocious interest in spiritual matters. With utmost candor, she was known to write, "I have never refused the good God anything."

This didn't mean she was immune to the moods and occasional expected tantrums of any young girl; after each storm, however, she returned to her union with divine love. She experienced a brief infatua-tion with a young man on the train to Rome, where she and her father were going on pilgrimage, and she admitted, "My heart is easily caught by tenderness . . . I am no different from others." But that heart wasn't distracted for long; it was set on entering Carmel.

She begged Pope Leo XIII to let her enter Carmel at age fifteen, but he told her that God's will had to be sought. In fact, she did enter the Lisieux Carmel shortly after that, and her brief years in the cloister were the proving ground for the heroic virtues she learned and practiced. She has been named a Doctor of the Church, for she has taught us by her life and words what Jesus meant when he said, "Unless you turn and become like children, you will never enter the kingdom of heaven" (Mt. 18:3).

All Is Grace — Especially for Homilists

Thérèse attributed all her strengths and insights to God's grace. The love of which she spoke was God's love, which she received with an open heart and shared joyfully with everyone. The pressures under which homilists work should remind them of their need of the graces that God so willingly gives us when we ask. Abraham Heschel put it this way: "All we own we owe." Our success in preaching depends on the power of the Holy Spirit awakening the hearts of those who hear us and prompting us to say the words that will touch them. All we own we owe, and all is grace.

It is a good practice to give God the glory after every homily, praising God for whatever good was done. The words of the psalmist need to be on the lips of every homilist, "Not to us, O LORD, not to us, but to thy name give glory" (cf. Ps.115). Humility not only endears us to our listeners but curbs the natural vanity that lures us to take all the credit for what we have said. Self-deprecation is the best medicine for the preacher.

This attitude is all the more attractive when preaching to children. Where else would Christ's wise words about becoming like a little child be more fitting than when speaking to them about the kingdom of God? The looks on their faces will tell us whether we have learned that truth or not. Children like to hear about God, and they can tell whether we mean what we say. Perhaps they can even, in some instinctive way, detect whether we know and love the God we preach. When we believe "all is grace," they will feel it, too.

Five Tips for Children's Homilies

Today, many parishes set aside a Liturgy of the Word, with a catechesis for children, in another setting than the church. The celebrant says a prayer for the catechists and the children and blesses them on their way to their own service.

I hope the spiritual attitudes taught by St. Thérèse influence the catechists; I think, however, that every so often, the children should remain for the regular Liturgy of the Word and the homily should be directed to them. This does not ignore the adults who, for the most part, enjoy hearing the faith expressed in the simple terms used for children. It is for these occasions the following tips are provided.

1. Do what you can to be involved with the children from the start. Get away from the lectern or pulpit and walk among the children, or gather the youngest children around you by the altar steps. Though the space between the lectern and altar is usually not vast, it is for them an invisible wall. A sense of closeness is important for communicating with them.

    - You might begin with some "powder-puff" questions, some things that get their hands up in the air, eager and ready to answer. Children love to answer fact questions.
    - One of the easiest ways to do this is to review the story of the Gospel. If it's the story of the paralytic being let down through the ripped-up roof of a private home, you can quickly involve them about what was done, and what the owner of the house would say. Then take them through questions about the forgiveness of the man's sins, the anger of the Pharisees, and the cure of his paralysis.
    - One of the secrets to children's preaching is that you are actually preaching to the adults, especially the parents. They eavesdrop on your dialogue.

2. Another way to get them involved is to tell them a story. You should avoid strange, bizarre stories, or "avenging God" tales. Don't try to scare them. Tell stories that illustrate how God loves them and wants them to be good, and show them how they can love God and others. Teach them both neighbor-loving and God-loving. It is often helpful to retell the reading from the Old Testament or the Gospel when there are a number of interesting background cultural details not mentioned in Scripture but fascinating, as well as helpful, for the children.

    Storytelling does not come easily to some priests, deacons, or bishops. I recommend that you think of how you talk over a cup of coffee with friends. You probably do not talk in full sentences or paragraphs. For example, notice how you retell what you thought was a bad call by a referee in yesterday's football game — how vividly and in close detail you repaint the picture. Almost everyone becomes a storyteller when the topic is dear to one's heart. Ask first-grade teachers about how they tell stories to children. Listen to the way children tell you their stories. Abstractions make the children's eyes glaze over. Stories open them again.

3. Go to your message for the day. You may want to use the children's lectionary, though this is not essential. You can recap the message from the day's readings in language familiar to the young. Use simple language in your homily, but don't be childish. Baby talk is out of place. Paradoxically, children like to be treated as "little adults."

4. Teach them lessons that encourage them to pray and to be helpful at home; to be good to their brothers and sisters and obedient to their parents; to play fair in games and make each other laugh; to stay clean and keep their rooms neat, to do their homework and listen to their teachers; to always tell the truth and be honest with everyone; to love God and their parents, brothers, sisters, friends, and neighbors — everyone.

5. Close with a small resolution for the children. Give them something to do. You might think of closing with a little two line poem that rhymes and has a strong beat — such as, "Jesus loves me, this I know, 'Cause the Bible tells me so." You can always make up your own little scriptural or ethical rhymes.

How have I improved my children's homilies?

St. Thérèse, pray that I be a better homilist for children.

It has been said, "Too soon old, too late smart." Yet those who remain close to the young become young at heart, no matter how old — and perhaps become smarter sooner.

SIXTEEN

Baptism Homilies

St. John the Baptist

I think it was more than a coincidence that God chose a preacher to give us the initial catechesis about Baptism. This was done by way of preparation by John the Baptist and quickly brought to fulfillment in the preaching of Christ. Prophetic preparation and Gospel fulfillment were found on the lips of preachers of the Word. The first of the sacraments was proclaimed by the words of the last prophet and the promised Messiah. Themes of repentance from sins, the promise of salvation, the institution of baptismal washing in water by John, and water and the Holy Spirit by Jesus, began their public ministries. John was the Voice who unrolls the scroll of prophecy. Jesus was the Word who endowed John's voice with its ultimate meaning in the saving sacrament of Baptism.

As a young man, John received the call from God to be a prophet, the first known prophet in Israel after 400 years. He was filled with the Holy Spirit in his mother's womb. He was a special blessing to his elderly parents, Zachary and Elizabeth. Emboldened by the Holy Spirit, he became a fiery prophet like a new Elijah. John finished the long cycle of prophets whom God had inspired from Elijah onwards.

He chose the desert for his living space, a center of solitude, an environment of prayer, a gymnasium for the soul. John loved to call himself "a voice crying out in the wilderness." St. Augustine was intrigued by John's self-description of a "voice" who prepared for the Messiah, whom Scripture would call the Word. A "voice" is important, but it is a temporary device. It is at the service of the word. Once the voice has done its duty, it goes into silence, but the word remains to affect our hearts and touch them with a movement to conversion.

> John is the voice, but the Lord is the *Word who was in the beginning*. John is the voice that lasts for a time; from the beginning

Christ is the Word who lives forever...When the word has been conveyed to you, does not the sound seem to say: *The Word ought to grow and I should diminish?* The sound of the voice has made itself heard in the service of the word, and has gone away, as though it were saying: *My joy is complete.* Let us hold onto the word, we must not lose the word conceived inwardly in our hearts.

— LITURGY OF THE HOURS, VOL. I, P. 261

When caravans paused in the desert at an oasis, John preached to them about the imminent coming of the Messiah. Using the Messianic language of Isaiah, he told them to prepare the way for the appearance of the Lord. Often, he also preached by the Jordan River to people headed for Jerusalem. To them he expanded his message to include baptism in the river waters: "Repent, for the kingdom of God is at hand. . . . I baptize you with water for repentance, but he who is coming after me is mightier than I . . . . he will baptize you with the Holy Spirit and with fire" (Mt. 3:2, 11).

Gradually, he attracted people from neighboring towns, called them to repentance and baptized them in the Jordan. The Gospel tells us that Jesus went to the Jordan to be baptized by John. John protests that he is not worthy to do this. Why would the all-holy one wish baptism? He is baptized not to be made holy but to make the water that would be used for our baptisms holy. St. Maximus of Turin draws these memorable comparisons from Christ's baptism:

At Christmas he was born from the Virgin; today he is born in mystery. When he was born a man, his mother Mary held him close to her heart: when he is born in mystery, God the Father embraces him with his voice when he says: *This is my beloved Son in whom I am well pleased.* The mother caresses the tender baby on her lap; the Father serves the Son by his loving testimony. The mother holds the child for the Magi to adore; the Father reveals that his Son is to be worshiped by all nations. That is why the Lord Jesus went to the river for baptism, that is why he wanted his holy body to be washed with Jordan's water.

— LITURGY OF THE HOURS, VOL. I, P. 612

PREACHING POINTS FOR A BAPTISM

- In Baptism, all sins are forgiven: original sin and all personal sins, as well as any punishment due to sin. But temporal consequences of sin remain in the baptized, such as illness, death, character weaknesses, and an inclination to sin.

- Baptism welcomes us into membership in the Church and the common priesthood of the faithful. We are joined to the body of Christ, the temple of the Spirit, and the people of God. This brings with it the responsibilities and rights of communion with the Church.

- By Word and Sacrament, prayers, and the witness of the believing community, each new member is nourished, strengthened, and sustained for the journey of faith. Baptism also unites us with other baptized people who are not yet in full communion with the Catholic Church. This serves as a bond with them as we work toward the unity of all believers desired by Christ.

- Baptism confers on us a "seal," an indelible spiritual "mark or character" that signifies our belonging to Christ. No sin can annul this. Once we are baptized, we stay baptized. The sacrament cannot be repeated.

- The word *baptism* comes from the Greek word that means "to plunge into water." The immersion in water symbolizes our death to sin. In emerging from the water, we rise with Christ to new life. We die with Christ and are reborn in him. Early Christians liked to call baptism the "enlightenment," because the revelatory teaching that accompanies the sacrament gives the light of Christ to our minds and hearts.

- The baptized are called to be active members of the Church and active participants in the sacraments, as well as enthusiastic witnesses to Christ by loving God and neighbor — especially in serving the poor and bringing the light of the Gospel to the society in which they live.

John the Baptist prepared for the arrival of the Messiah and initiated the preliminaries of the sacrament of Baptism. For this reason, I select him to be the patron of our homilies for this sacrament.

"The Lord himself affirms that Baptism is necessary for salvation (cf. Jn. 3:5) . . . Baptism is necessary for salvation for those to whom the Gospel has been proclaimed and who have had the possibility of asking for this sacrament" (*CCC* 1257).

Just before his Ascension into heaven, Jesus gave the apostles the Great Commission to preach the Gospel and baptize the converts. "Go therefore and make disciples of all nations, baptizing them in the name of the Father and of the Son and of the Holy Spirit" (Mt. 28:19–20).

The Liturgy of Baptism

The rite of baptism has varied throughout history, but six essential elements have always been present:

(1) the proclamation of the Word
(2) a religious conversion that included acceptance of the Gospel
(3) the profession of faith
(4) the baptism itself
(5) the receiving of the Holy Spirit
(6) admission to Eucharist.

In the early Church, the candidacy for adults involved a number of stages that included religious instruction and various rituals. In the case of babies, such a process was impossible beforehand, so there was need for a catechetical explanation after the child was old enough to understand. Vatican II has restored the catechumenate, the process for initiating converts into the Church.

The meaning of baptism is best seen through the ceremonies by which it is celebrated. The Rite contains six rituals that teach us baptism's significance:

1. *Sign of the Cross.* The imprint of the Cross on the candidate reminds us of Christ's sacrifice by which he saved us. Baptism is a sacrament of salvation from sin and the gift of divine life.
2. *Readings from Scripture.* God's revealed Word is spoken to the candidate with the purpose of asking for a faith response, a faith

that implies conversion to Christ and obedience to his Word. Baptism is a sacrament of faith.

3. *Exorcism and Anointing.* Jesus is about to liberate the candidate from evil. An exorcism prayer is recited to loosen the power of Satan over the catechumen; then, the celebrant anoints him or her with the Oil of Catechumens. The candidate explicitly renounces Satan and professes the faith of the Church.

4. *The Essential Rite of Baptism.* The candidate is either immersed three times in water, or water is poured three times upon the head. The celebrant says, "N., I baptize you in the name of the Father and of the Son and of the Holy Spirit." This brings about death to all sin, original and personal, and entry into the life of the Trinity through identity with Christ's paschal mystery.

5. *Anointing with Chrism.* The celebrant anoints the newly baptized with oil of chrism to symbolize the person's internal anointing and reception of the Holy Spirit.

6. *Invest with White Garment and Candle.* The white garment shows that the baptized has put on Jesus and risen with him. The candle symbolizes the light of Christ which the baptized person has now received.

These ceremonies are teachers of the meaning of baptism, not just in terms of the words that are spoken, but also in the nonverbal elements. Now, the newly baptized is an adopted child of God in union with Jesus and able to pray, "Our Father."

Baptism is God's most beautiful and magnificent gift. . . . We call it gift, grace, anointing, enlightenment, garment of immortality, bath of rebirth, seal and most precious gift. It is called *gift* because it is conferred on those who bring nothing of their own; *grace* since it is given even to the guilty; *Baptism* because sin is buried in the water; *anointing* for it is priestly and royal as are those who are anointed; *enlightenment* because it radiates light; *clothing* since it veils our shame; *bath* because it washes; *seal* as it is our guard and the sign of God's Lordship.

— St. Gregory of Nazienzus, *Oratio 40*, 3–4

What have been my most inspiring Baptism homilies?

St. John the Baptist, pray that I minister in deep faith at Baptisms.

The Church is not about satisfying expectations, but celebrating the mysteries.

— Cardinal Carlo Maria Martini

SEVENTEEN

Advent Homilies

Isaiah: prophet of the Advent

The Church chooses Isaiah to be a prophet for the season of Advent. The Scripture lessons from the Office of Readings are almost all from Isaiah as are many of the weekday readings in the Masses. What is his story? Born in Jerusalem about the year 762 B.C., he grew up in a family that trained him to have a sense of justice. His parents educated him to oppose the immoral treatment of the poor by selfish rich people.

They told him about vicious loan sharks. They showed him how some businessmen cheated customers with false weights and measures. They held family discussions about the prevalence of bribery at King Uzziah's court, the corruption of certain priests and the helplessness of the poor. With his parents he studied the Bible and absorbed the message of the covenant. His parents gave him a moral and religious conscience.

On his twenty-first birthday, he received an invitation to the enthronement of King Jotham. Amid the splendor of music, incense, processions, and the purple-robed king, Isaiah had a profound mystical experience. He later wrote: "I saw the Lord" (Is 6:1). In his vision, he saw the figure of God on a throne, surrounded by angels who sang of the holiness of God. The scene filled him with awe and with a sense of his own unworthiness, so far removed from the purity and holiness of God.

> And I said: "Woe is me! For I am lost; for I am a man of unclean lips, and I dwell in the midst of a people of unclean lips; for my eyes have seen the King, the LORD of hosts!" Then flew one of the seraphim to me, having in his hand a burning coal which he had taken with tongs from the altar. And he touched my mouth, and said, "Behold, this has touched your lips; your guilt is taken away, and your sin forgiven."
>
> — Is. 6:5–7

Then, Isaiah heard God say he had a mission and wondered who would be willing to accept it. Isaiah replied, "Here am I! Send me" (Is. 6:8). He had gone to the enthronement as a conscientious young man. He walked away from the Temple grounds as a new prophet, one of the greatest who would ever live. For nearly fifty years he preached and witnessed the holiness of God and the need for justice in the land. He spoke truth to power but found that the rulers paid little attention.

Isaiah began to see that no ruler in his lifetime would really bring God's holiness and justice to the people. The prophet began to realize that the advent of a messiah in the future would be God's response to this need. He soon experienced visions and dreams of what that would be like. These occurred during his "ministry of silence" in the reign of Hezekiah, a king who did improve matters somewhat.

Out of that contemplative silence, Isaiah produced remarkable poetic descriptions of the messianic times and what the messiah would do. Handel's *Messiah* put his messianic prophecies to music so exalted that it is as linked to the Christmas season as are the carols. In it are his dreams of the peaceable kingdom, the shepherd who would feed his flock, the virgin who would conceive and give birth to the messiah, the coming of the glory of the Lord, and the appearance of the "child."

> For to us a child is born, to us a son is given; and the government will be upon his shoulder, and his name will be called "Wonderful Counselor, Mighty God, Everlasting Father, Prince of Peace."
>
> — Is. 9:6

Many of his prophecies read like a Christmas gospel. His writings are perfectly suited to the Christian Advent. He formed a school of prophets to carry on his message of hope. Like him, they would follow his wisdom in their sermons, "Comfort, comfort my people, says your God. Speak tenderly to Jerusalem, and cry to her that her warfare is ended, that her iniquity is pardoned" (Is. 40:1–2).

Recover the *Kerygma* in Your Preaching

"Names make news" is one of the first principles of the mass media. Of all the names that outlast temporary stars of the movies, politics, philosophy, science, and popular novelists, Jesus Christ has the greatest name recognition. So the name of Jesus appears frequently in our time. In a secular sense, he is a "Superstar." But the "Superstar" is rarely the real Jesus. His name is invoked to serve other agendas, none of which call for faith in him. Here are a few examples:

- *Harper's* magazine, December 2005, featured a cover story called "Jesus Without Miracles." The article described Thomas Jefferson's "Gospel," in which he cut out all supernatural material — miracles, virgin birth, resurrection — and kept only the sayings of Jesus. This reduces Christ to a moral teacher and eliminates his mission as a Savior.
- The celebrated novel *The Da Vinci Code* portrays Jesus as marrying Mary Magdalene, having children, and siring a dynasty. This Jesus is human but not divine.
- In the film *The Last Temptation of Christ,* Jesus seems to have no idea of his messianic purpose or mission and fantasizes marrying Mary Magdalene. Here again is a cultural Christ, but not a scriptural one.

These rationalized versions of Jesus require no faith from us. In many ways, these approaches of the post-Christian world parallel the confusions of the pre-Christian world that the Apostolic preachers set out to convert. In a series of Advent sermons to the papal household, Fr. Rainiero Cantalamesa recovers the strategy of the apostles facing a pre-Christian world. What can preachers today learn from them?

He distinguishes two forms of the sermons of the apostles. The first he calls *Kerygma*: the announcing of the salvation brought to us by Jesus Christ, who was born of the Virgin Mary by the power of the Holy Spirit, died to save us from our sins, and rose from the dead to offer us the gift of divine life. This leads us to praise him with the title, "Jesus is Lord." This is a divine revelation that appeals to our hearts and calls us to faith. This is the sun that illumines the birth of faith. It is original dream of Christianity.

The second kind of sermons they delivered were *Didache*, or teachings about the moral and spiritual conduct of those who have declared their faith in Christ. They showed how the commandments of Jesus and his various moral teachings were practical outcomes of their commitment to Christ. These matters give form to faith and help preserve its purity. But it is the power of the *Kerygma* that awakens faith. It is more like the seed that produces the tree rather than the fruit the tree yields. If our church labors under its immense patrimony of doctrines, laws, and institutions, it may reach the point where the *kerygma* that awakens faith is effectively lost.

> We are more prepared by our past to be "shepherds" than to be "fishers" of men. We are better prepared to nourish the people that come to church than to bring new people to church, or to catch those who have fallen away and live outside her. This is one of the reasons why in some parts of the world many Catholics leave the Catholic Church for other Christian realities. They are attracted by a simple and effective announcement that puts them in direct contact with Christ and makes them experience the power of the Spirit.
>
> — RAINIERO CANTALAMESA,
> "FAITH IN CHRIST TODAY AND AT THE BEGINNING OF THE CHURCH,"
> REPRINTED FROM HIS WEB SITE

Four Prominent Homiletic Themes of Advent

(1) The Second Coming

As the majestic hymn for Advent proclaims for us: "Lo, he comes with clouds descending . . . Thousand thousand saints attending . . . Swell the triumph of his reign . . . God appears on earth to reign." Advent begins with its eyes on the end time when Christ will return in glory to judge the living and the dead and mysteriously transform the heavens and the earth. This is a Catholic teaching that is rarely preached yet is filled with hope and glory. All the Gospels for the first Sundays of Advent are from Christ's Last Judgment Sermons. Link these with the description of Christ in glory from Rev. 19 and the New Heavens and New Earth of Rev. 21–22.

(SEE *THE SECOND COMING OF JESUS*,
ALFRED MCBRIDE, O. PRAEM., OUR SUNDAY VISITOR;
REVERSED THUNDER, EUGENE PETERSON, HARPER COLLINS)

(2) *Call to Conversion*

The Gospels portray the ministry of John the Baptist who echoes the expectations of Isaiah about the Messiah that requires repentance, conversion, and baptism with water. This basically calls for a *Kerygma* style of homily, with its fundamental invitation to get ready for faith in Christ through a spiritual and moral change.

(3) *Rejoice Heartily in the Lord*

Show your people how the Gospel is the Good News of salvation. With Pope John XXIII, help them to push aside the prophets of gloom, to announce that God is Love, to see the Church's role as offering the medicine of mercy and not the severity of condemnation. "For God sent the Son into the world, not to condemn the world, but that the world might be saved through him" (Jn. 3:17).

(4) *Virgin Mary — Mother of God*

The Gospels dwell on Mary's Annunciation, Visitation, and her dilemma with Joseph, until it was solved by the angel. The Church leads us to contemplate the Holy Spirit's powerful work in the life of Mary and her inspiring faith and trust in God that results in her giving birth to Jesus. Set before our eyes just before Christmas, these Marian events are excellent sources of faith growth in us and our people.

As we prepare to receive the Christ Child anew in this season of Advent, our faith compels us to hear the cry of all children, especially poor children. We must remember that every day millions of children are born suffering from hunger and poverty. Many of them will die of preventable disease.

If we are to receive the Christ Child fully into our hearts, we must allow the Holy Spirit to work fully within us and shape our lives. We are called to take on God's passionate concern for the

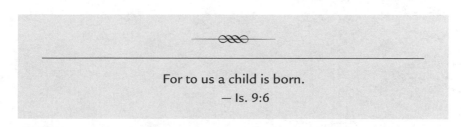

For to us a child is born.
— Is. 9:6

world's poor and oppressed people. This Advent and Christmas, let us remember with Isaiah that the Child who "brings light to those who walk in darkness" tells us that "if we offer food to the hungry and satisfy the needs of the afflicted," our own "light shall rise in the darkness" and our "gloom shall be like the noonday" (Is. 58).

— FROM *BREAD FOR THE WORLD* WEB SITE

Which of my Advent homilies have been proven to be the most effective?

Dear Isaiah and John the Baptist, pray that I may deliver better Advent homilies.

EIGHTEEN

Christmas Homilies

St. Norbert (1080–1134): began his Order on Christmas Day

The Church of the eleventh century teemed with reforms. Pope Gregory VII (Hildebrand) set about eliminating the practice of lay investiture, meaning the lay control of the selection of bishops. Bernard of Clairvaux and the Cistercians revolutionized the monastic world with a return to the primitive practice of the Rule of St. Benedict. Norbert of Xanten — a town near the Dutch-German border — led a movement to improve the spiritual and pastoral lives of the parish clergy.

Norbert did not begin his young adult life as a reformer. He was an easygoing man, more interested in pleasure than the pursuit of higher ideals. He was ordained a deacon to serve in the local cathedral, where he was called to chant the Liturgy of the Hours with the canons. Then, Emperor Henry V appointed him as one of his chaplains in the royal court in Cologne. The salary enabled him to live the pleasurable style of the local nobility.

During a trip to Rome with the emperor, Norbert experienced the beginning of a moral conversion. He witnessed a breakdown in the negotiations between the emperor and the pope over the lay investiture issue. He saw the pope stand firm on the principle that it was wrong for the secular power to select bishops. It gave the impression that sacramental ministry came from a secular power and tended to corrupt those bishops.

Norbert's moral awakening was accentuated when he was nearly killed by a bolt of lightning during a storm, and he entered the abbey of Siburg for a lengthy self-evaluation. After three years of prayer and self-scrutiny, he presented himself for priesthood and a commitment to the ideals of Jesus and the Gospels. He asked, and received, from the pope a personal mandate to preach repentance, peace, and moral reform in France. He mediated peace among the numerous battles of the warlords. In village after village, he found armed combat and hatred, and he struggled for peace. He also encountered a demoralized clergy, lonely and feeling neglected by the Church. He did what he could to encourage them and improve their morale.

In the year 1120, he was working in the diocese of Bishop Bartholomew of Laon. The bishop convinced him that his influence would be far greater if he founded a religious order. He was persuaded to found a community of priests whose formation would occur in a monastic setting. Their common life would center on the celebration of the Eucharist and the Liturgy of the Hours, along with practicing the vows of poverty, chastity, and obedience, and a vowed dedication to the community. They imagined themselves like a new creation of the communities of the "apostolic life," as described in Acts 2:42–47.

The Magi saw a heavenly wonder and believed it announced the birth of a heavenly person. Thousands of others saw the same wonder but did not come to the same conclusion. Herod saw the star but paid no attention. Why were the wise men so wise? Because they understood that believing can be seeing. Herod said, "Show me a sign, then I will believe." In the Rock opera *[Jesus Christ] Superstar*, Herod sang, "Prove to me that you're no fool, walk across my swimming pool. Prove to me that you're divine, change this water into wine." Herod wanted proof before he would believe. The Magi reversed the process. Believe in the Lord and he will show you a sign of his presence. These scientists of the stars were not blinded by their rational calculations. They did not stop being scientists in order to believe. They believed and remained good scientists.

Church Fathers were fond of pointing out that Jesus is first revealed to the poor and humble shepherds, then later to the prosperous Magi from Persia. Chesterton noted that Jesus disclosed himself to the humble who knew they knew little and then to the learned who appreciated they did not know everything. Finding Jesus today requires the simplicity of the shepherds and the wondering, inquiring minds of the Magi.

— Fr. Alfred McBride, *Year of the Lord, Cycle B*, p. 20

The difference between his monasteries and others is that his members would be priests, destined to engage in pastoral ministries — unlike the others, whose non-ordained monks were primarily devoted to the contemplative life. Norbert's group would be Canons (priests) Regular (living in community under the Rule of St. Augustine). Eventually, the Order admitted lay brothers. The dream came true on Christmas Day 1121 when the little group professed their vows in the small chapel of St. John the Baptist in the valley of Premontre. The feast of Christmas infused this new community with the spirit of the Incarnation, an attitude that sought to imitate the Son of God who was willing to become a man and walk among us. It is a humane vision that has endured for over eight centuries.

Norbert's ministerial style was wedded to his gift of preaching. "He was a most eloquent preacher. After long meditation he would preach the Word of God and with his fiery eloquence purged vices, refined virtues and filled the souls of good will with the warmth of wisdom" (LITURGY OF THE HOURS, Vol. III, p. 1459). Norbert's vision resulted in the founding of numerous abbeys and priories over many centuries, and today, his heirs may be found on every continent.

And the Word Was Made Flesh

When the time had fully come, God sent forth his Son, born of woman, born under the law, to ransom those who were under the law, so that we might receive adoption.

— GAL. 4:4–5

In many and various ways God spoke of old to our fathers by prophets; but in these last days he has spoken to us by a Son, whom he appointed the heir of all things, through whom also he created the world.

— HEB. 1:1–2

Christ Jesus emptied himself and took the form of a slave. He was tested like us in all things and did not sin. Now let us worship him with deep faith.

— EVENING PRAYER I, INTERCESSION

Christian, remember your dignity, and now that you share in God's own nature, do not return by sin to your former base condition. Bear in mind who is your head and of whose body you are a member. Do not forget you have been rescued from the power of darkness and brought into the light of God's kingdom.

— St. Leo the Great, Christmas Homily

Ten Christmas Truths — Seeds of Meditation for Homilies

1. The eternal Son of God was born a man of the Virgin Mary, who conceived him by the power of the Holy Spirit. Jesus Christ came into the world and heralded the new age foretold by the prophets.

2. Jesus assumed the weakness of the human condition, being born in poverty and humility so that he could lead all of us into his kingdom of salvation, love, justice, and mercy.

3. Angels appeared to shepherds the night Jesus was born and told them news of great joy — that the Savior of the world had been born for them and all peoples. The child is little, yet called mighty God.

4. In Bible times, it was customary for musicians to come to a home where a new birth occurred and sing a welcome to the newborn baby. In the field of the shepherds, the angels sang the first Christmas carol, "Glory to God in the highest, and on earth peace" (Lk. 2:14).

5. The shepherds adored the divine and human child. They gazed at the mystery of Christ. Angels guided their perceptions. They saw a God who held the world in his hands yet could scarcely enfold the heads of the cattle. They beheld the source of life turn to his mother's breast for the milk of survival. Reality's greatest free spirit put up with the annoyances of human limits.

6. If we forget the God in the cave, we reduce the Bethlehem event to a charming birth scene with no eternal meaning. But if we forget the human and only see God, we would endow the occasion with the aura of magic and myth and rob it of any historical or salvation truth. Christmas is not Christmas if these paradoxes — seeming contradictions — are denied or ignored.

7. Some people would settle for singing nursery rhymes at Christ's cradle. The shepherd hummed the song of the angels about the arrival of Christ the Lord. The maternal in us simply wants to rock the cradle; with the shepherds, we believe this cradle will rock the world.

8. The ancient Romans built a pantheon for all the gods of the world. They invited Christians to put a statue of Jesus there with the other gods. "Be open-minded," they said. "Join the fellowship of world religions." The Christians said, "No, thanks. Jesus alone is the world's only Lord and Savior."

9. Almighty God and Father of light, a child is born for us and a son is given to us. Your eternal Word leaped down from heaven in the silent watches of the night. And now your Church is filled with wonder at the nearness of our God. Open our hearts to receive his life and increase our vision with the rising of dawn.

    — CHRISTMAS LITURGY OF HOURS, ALTERNATIVE PRAYER

10. We gaze at the humility of Jesus and pray that our pride will melt away. We behold his infinite purity and yearn that our weakened nature will be reborn. We sense his everlasting tranquility and beg him to flood our hearts with peace. We contemplate a God who has accepted the limits of the earthly condition, and we open ourselves to an honest embrace of life's boundaries. We pray with the shepherds, "O hold Jesus tenderly, dear mother, for he rules our hearts."

Write out your list of ten Christmas themes for homilies.

Savior, I greet you on this Christmas morning.
Jesus, to thee be all glory given.
Word of the Father, now in flesh appearing.
O come, let us adore him.

Today the Magi gaze in deep wonder at what they see: God in man, one whom the whole universe cannot contain now enclosed in a tiny body. As they look they believe and do not question, as their symbolic gifts bear witness: incense for God, gold for a king, myrrh for one who is to die.

— St. Peter Chrysologus, Liturgy of the Hours,
Vol. I, p. 578

NINETEEN

How to Deliver a Homily

St. Francis de Sales: under the radar

For a modern Church finding itself in the midst of a communications revolution, St. Francis de Sales looms as a friendly and encouraging figure. He was wise enough to take advantage of the comparatively new print medium of his time and put it at the service of evangelization. He understood the dynamics of his culture in which a raging struggle went on between Protestants and Catholics as a result of the Reformation. He was perceptive enough to notice how Jesus Christ might be communicated in a fresh new manner.

Born in 1567 to an upper-middle-class family in the province of Savoy, Francis was sent to study law at the University of Padua with the idea that he would enter local politics and run for the senate. Francis did not want a career in politics, however. Instead, he became a priest and, ultimately, the bishop of Geneva. In those turbulent times, the religion of the people normally seesawed between Catholic and Protestant, depending on the religion of political ruler. But when a Catholic ruler took over in Savoy, the prevailing Protestant majority refused to change their faith; missionary priests and bishops were needed to bring the people back to the Catholic fold.

At first, Francis followed the traditional tactic of moving from town to town, visiting Catholic families to encourage them and using their homes as bases from which to reach out to Calvinists. But he soon found this process slow, frustrating, and inefficient. Not enough people were being touched on a regular and persuasive basis. Then, Francis discovered what Luther had already known and mastered — namely, the power of the print medium to spread ideas, change hearts, and convert people.

So Francis became a pamphleteer; this print medium had been around for over a century but was scarcely used by the Church, except for St. Peter Canisius, whose printed catechism was phenomenally successful. Francis began writing what amounted to a weekly newsletter containing a point of Catholic doctrine in simple, lucid prose, along with arguments against the Calvinist positions. His enormous number of writings has earned him the title of Patron of Journalists by the Church.

His Preaching Delivery

In addition, Francis found within himself another unsuspected talent: he happened to be an unusually appealing public speaker. His training in classics supplied him with the abundant imagery of their poets, his legal training with the arts of persuasion. But he was unique in his decision to adopt a low-key, laid-back speaking style, in contrast to the pretentious fulminations of the preachers of his time. Francis had the common touch and a sure sense of where his audience was, as well as the poet's gift of choosing down-home comparisons — as is evident in his oft-

As a writer, St. Francis de Sales was aware of the diversity of his readers and their individual needs. His success as a preacher flowed from the same appreciation of the differences among his listeners.

I say that devotion must be practiced in different ways by the nobleman and by the working man, by the servant and by the prince, by the widow and the unmarried girl and by the married woman. But even this distinction is not sufficient, for the practice of devotion must be adapted to the strength, to the occupation and the duties of each one in particular. Tell me please, my Philothea, whether it is proper for a Bishop to lead a solitary life like a Carthusian; or for married people to be no more concerned than a Capuchin about increasing their income, or for a working man to spend his whole day in church like a religious; or on the other hand for a religious to be constantly exposed like a bishop to all the events and circumstances that bear on the needs of our neighbor. Is not this sort of devotion ridiculous, unorganized and intolerable?

— *Introduction to Devout Life*, Part 1, Chapter 3

quoted advice about motivation, "a spoonful of honey works better than a barrel of vinegar."

His conversational speaking style is the kind looked for in today's TV presenters: relaxed and natural, pungent without being pugnacious, a capacity to be critical of an opposition without being too shrill or strident. He delivered thousands of sermons in this manner in countless cities and towns. His calm speaking style and sweet soft-sell approach have led many commentators to speak mellifluously of the "gentle de Sales." But this is a misleading characterization, for it implied that Francis was a sentimentalist; in fact, he was more a contained volcano than a pitcher of syrup.

His style was "gentle" only in contrast with the angry polemics and theatrical posturing common in his day. He was a self-assured speaker who resolutely repudiated power plays against the congregation because he believed in their inner hunger to hear the truth and their immense satisfaction when they heard it.

His thirty-year ministry as priest and bishop in the Lake Geneva area broke the Calvinist ascendancy. He permitted himself a slight (and forgivable) exaggeration when he said, "When we arrived here, were not more than fifteen Catholics in the area of my ministry, and now there are not more than fifteen Calvinists."

Under the Radar

The arrival of good sound systems and microphones in most of our churches has put aside the need to shout to be heard or the tendency to use flamboyant gestures to score a point. However, acoustics are still a problem in many churches. This puts a strain on the homilist who struggles to be heard and understood. One thing I notice is that some homilists and readers expect the sound system to carry all the burden. The biggest error is failing to project one's voice, something that requires opening one's mouth, breathing from the diaphragm, lifting up one's voice, and sending it out. Speech teachers say you should throw your voice against the back wall. This is not the same as yelling which is harmful to your voice and painful for your listeners. At the same time, it is necessary to talk through the microphone, not above it nor below it. Of course, if you are using a lavaliere microphone, it generally picks up your voice, so long as it is strategically attached.

CARDINAL RATZINGER'S HOMILY AT JOHN PAUL'S FUNERAL

Perhaps the most indelible memory for anyone who experienced the homily was the way the crowd, quite literally, **became Ratzinger's conversation partner.** At first, Ratzinger seemed startled by the applause, but quickly he learned to wait for it, not to proceed until the mourners had been heard. Repeatedly the crowd broke out into strong and deep chants, *santo subito*, sainthood now!
— John Allen, *The Rise of Benedict XVI*. Doubleday, 2005; p. 66

TV has changed the way people expect good communication to be. They like its conversational style. They accept the wide use of the talk show as a popular forum. They are accustomed to condensed news and opinions as sound bites. They welcome the feeling that a friend is talking to them and confiding information, advice, cautions, humor, or some pithy wisdom. TV has connected public speaking with intimacy. Its messages come through "under the radar," rather than by blunt trauma.

The modern homilist needs to learn these lessons in delivery. Most people spend at least twenty hours a week watching TV. The homilist has about twelve minutes a week to reach them and match the delivery skills of well-paid communicators.

A Checklist for Your Homiletic Delivery:

- Use the sound system intelligently.
- Project your voice by opening your mouth, breathing from your diaphragm, and sending your voice to the whole assembly.
- Do not shout or yell; it harms your voice.
- Talk in a conversational manner.
- Take it easy and don't rush. The bigger your church, the more you need to slow down, let the sound (and the meaning) reach the ears and minds of your people.

- Acquire a sense of intimacy with your listeners. Don't talk *at* them. Talk *with* them, as though you were having a cup of coffee together.
- Imagine you were having dinner with them. How would you pass your message on to them?
- When you watch talk shows on TV, notice how the host speaks and involves the guests.
- Look at your congregation. Find a friendly face to get confidence, and then scan the group. Preaching is a communion with your people. Even though you do all the talking, it is an implicit dialogue. Their attentiveness sparks your creativity.
- Send your message "under the radar." Stories and images do this for you. The less "pushy" you sound, the more likely your message will slip past their defenses, especially on controversial moral issues . . . and even issues of Truth.
- Convey your respect for your people — even your love. This should develop after you have been with a given parish for about a year.
- Sound like a friend and not a boss — or an "authority." You may in a sense be both, but people do not like to be reminded of it. If you are naturally pompous, take a course in humility. Check with your spiritual director.
- Stop reading so much from your text or your notes. Lovers don't read their sweet nothings to one another. Friends don't carry a text to carry on a conversation.
- Be yourself and do your best.
- Finally, follow the universal advice of all homiletics teachers: Prepare. Prepare. Prepare.

How can I improve my homiletic delivery?

Lord Jesus, help me to preach better, briefer, boldly.

A passionate preacher is one who helps the assembly get closer to God and become more aware of how God is reconciling all people to himself and each other.

Lenten Homilies

Sr. Thea Bowman, F.S.P.A. (1937–1990): she lived the mystery
of the Cross

S r. Thea Bowman was an accomplished preacher, filled with faith in Jesus and a passionate love for God and humanity, and brought the joy of the Gospel to thousands of people. At the height of her health and powers, Sr. Thea made more than 100 appearances each year, giving lectures, recitals, short courses, workshops, and conference presentations. She spread Christ's message that people are important and gifted, that "Black is beautiful," and that the Church needed to help Blacks get a good education.

She brought this message to the U.S. bishops on June 17, 1989, at the meeting at Seton Hall University. Suffering from bone cancer, she spoke from a wheelchair. Here's what she said about Catholic schools:

> I've got to say one more thing. You-all ain't going to like this but that's all right. The Church has repeatedly asked black folk, what do you want, what can the Church do for you? And black folk all over the country are saying, help us to education. We need education. The way out of poverty is education. We can't be Church without education because ignorance kills and cripples us. Black people are still asking the Church for education.

The bishops received her words with approval and warmth. When she finished her talk, she asked them to join her in singing *We Shall Overcome* with their arms joined to bring them closer together. She often said, "We do not want to change the theology of the Church, we just want to express this theology within the roots of Black spiritual culture."

Boston College honored Sr. Thea with an honorary degree, Doctor of Religion, in 1989. She was the first African-American woman to receive a Doctorate of Religion from Boston College. The citation emphasized her spiritual power and the effectiveness of her preaching:

> In the glory of your ministry we witness the Franciscan ideal of joy rendered more radiant by a woman of lively, living faith, truly Black and authentically Catholic. To your lifetime of building the Kingdom of God, preaching the Good News in the language of your people, and reclaiming the virtues and values that are your inheritance, Boston College says an approving "Amen!" and proudly declares you Doctor of Religion.

Sr. Thea Bowman was born in Canton, Mississippi, on December 19, 1937. Her grandfather was a slave, her father a physician, and her mother a teacher. Thea was raised as a Methodist until, at age nine, she asked her parents if she could become a Catholic. At age fifteen, she joined the Franciscan Sisters of Perpetual Adoration in La Crosse, Wisconsin. She earned a B.A. in English and Drama from Viterbo College and doctorates in English Literature and Linguistics from the Catholic University of America.

After sixteen years of teaching at the elementary, secondary, and college levels, she accepted an appointment from the Bishop of Jackson, Mississippi, as a Consultant for Intercultural Awareness. She worked with young people to raise their awareness of their gifts and cultural inheritance. Through song, dance, poetry, drama, story, and inspirational preaching, she communicated to them — and to teachers — joy, freedom, and pride, using traditional Black teaching techniques that were holistic and called for participation.

Even as she was dying, she remained as active as she could in her ministry. She lived her "Way of the Cross" in full sight of others, showing them that suffering is part of life. Her personal witness to the paschal mystery made her sermons, stories, songs, and poems acquire a reality that words alone seldom achieve.

On March 30, 1990, Sr. Thea Bowman died at age 52. Veteran journalist Mike Wallace had interviewed her for a *60 Minutes* profile in 1987. Wallace later wrote, "I don't remember when I've been more moved, more enchanted by anyone." And she is a Lenten inspiration for homilists.

The faith is not spread by pundits or even teachers, but by teachers who are witnesses. Martyr means witness. When I was a young priest I had the privilege of meeting Archbishop Oscar Romero. I spent a month with him in Puebla . . . A few days before his death he said, "I have frequently been threatened with death. Martyrdom is a grace from God that I do not believe I have earned, but you can tell them that if they succeed in killing me that I pardon them, but I wish they could realize they are wasting their time. A bishop will die, but the Church will never die." On March 24, 1980, Archbishop Romero was killed while celebrating Mass. As he fell with the consecrated chalice his blood was mixed with the blood of Christ.

The pulpit is the important arena of our martyrdom, of our witnessing. It can be painful. It can be frustrating. But it can also produce much fruit . . . The Good News must be preached with clarity. No one will follow an uncertain trumpet blast. The Gospel must be preached with a compelling sense of urgency and a profound trust in God and hope in his words.

— Archbishop Sean O'Malley,
"Why Preaching Must Be a Priority Today,"
Origins, April 22, 2004

"Pass the Cross to Me"

One of the most moving songs in the musical *Shenandoah* is the revival hymn, "Pass the Cross to Me." This is a theme that suits the season of Lent well, with its annual focus on the mystery of salvation in terms of the Cross and Easter. In the heady days after the close of Vatican II, it was the fashion to dwell mainly on Easter, just as before the Council there was an almost exclusive emphasis on the Cross. We are now in a better position to view the unity of the paschal mystery. There is no Easter without a Good Friday.

The Risen Christ was not ashamed to retain the wounds of his historical passion. The historical Christ was bold enough to speak of his forthcoming Easter. As the German theologian Moltmann said, we preach a "Crucified God." Nothing dilutes the message of salvation more than to ignore the Cross or to so smother it with roses and "nice thoughts" that its value and meaning vanish. All great saints and missionaries have attributed their effectiveness to their fidelity to the "Word of the Cross." The self-emptying, self-discipline, and self-giving that characterize the Cross are absolute prerequisites for Easter.

Lenten Themes . . . Homiletic Seeds from Cycle A

First Sunday:

- Draw attention to the narrative of the Fall of Man. The mystery of salvation is God's response to this. Self-salvation is impossible. Only God could deliver us from evil.
- The first Adam failed to resist temptation. The second Adam resisted the triple temptation in the desert. We learn to overcome temptation — inspired by Christ's example and strengthened by the graces he won for us.
- Tradition teaches us that prayer, fasting, and almsgiving are ideal methods for Lenten penance and spiritual conversion.

Second Sunday:

- Jesus revealed his inner glory to Peter, James and John to arouse their faith in him and give them a foretaste of his resurrection. The Father reconfirms his love for his Son.
- God is mystery but he wills to reveal himself. The psalms say that clouds and thick darkness surround him. This is mystery. His lightnings light up the world. The earth sees and adores. This is his revelation (see Ps. 97:2–4).

Third Sunday:

- The conversion of the Samaritan woman occurs through the patient compassion of Jesus for her salvation. Jesus begins the process by establishing a trusting relationship with her.
- Only then did he move to the next stage and confront her with her moral problems. Her moment of truth opens her heart.

- Lastly, Jesus leads her to be aware of her need for salvation and, at the same time, reveal to her that he is the Messiah she seeks. Most conversions are incremental and not dramatic.

Fourth Sunday:

- Physical blindness is often used as a metaphor for mental stubbornness and spiritual sin. We naturally feel compassion for the physically blind, but we find it frustrating to empathize with closed minds and hearts, such as found in the religious leaders in today's Gospel.
- Blindness in religion, either from its leaders or supposedly devout members, causes prophets to be stoned and angels to weep. Jesus is our light.

Fifth Sunday:

- The resurrection of Lazarus is a testimony to Christ being our life as well as our light. It is also a promise of Christ's resurrection and our own.
- In the creed we say, "I believe in the resurrection of the [my] body." At death, life is changed, not taken away. At the Last Judgment, our bodies will rise again. Jesus is our life.

Sixth Sunday:

- Holy Week begins with Christ's triumphal entry into Jerusalem. People waved palm branches and sang, "Hosanna to the Son of David." On Good Friday, their cheers will become jeers.
- At the end of the Last Supper, Jesus sang praises to his Father, just as he began his path to the Cross. Christian martyrs sang hymns of praise to Christ on their way into the Roman arena.
- The paradox of facing death with faith is that it draws from the dark jaws of apparent defeat the most astounding victories of the human spirit.

What will be the substance of my witnessing this Lent?

I adore you, O Christ, and I praise you, for by your Cross and Resurrection you have redeemed the world, and through Baptism, the Holy Eucharist, and the other sacraments, you have given us the fruits of your saving acts.

We need to break open the Word of God on our knees.

— Archbishop O'Malley

TWENTY-ONE

Preaching Easter

Cardinal Joseph Bernardin (1928–1996): he witnessed the Risen Lord

Cardinal Bernardin learned the truth that his life of faith was a process in which the journey was as important as the destination. How he lived was essentially bound up with where he was going.

In his memoir, *The Gift of Peace*, he used the images from the Stations of the Cross to mark out key moments in his life that were leading him to the gift of Easter faith. He freely shared his anxieties, especially his three fears: that he would be falsely accused, that he would die before his mother did, and that he would perish from cancer.

When these fears materialized, however, they became stepping stones of deeper surrender to God. He bore the Cross, but not morosely or with self-pity. He lived Christ's invitation to assume a burden and discovered it was light when Christ carried it with him. He wore the yoke of the Savior and found it was sweet, as Jesus predicted.

His use of the Stations imagery was just right, because Christ chose to suffer and die in public. Christ's indignities were not hidden, whether they happened in a courtroom, in the court of Pilate, before a mob, being paraded in public through the streets, or on a very visible cross.

Bernardin did not hide his embarrassments. When falsely accused, he called a press conference and denied the accusation. When his accuser recanted, Bernardin forgave him immediately and, later, went to visit him and anoint him. When the cardinal received news of his cancer and went to the hospital for therapy, he was offered a private entrance used for dignitaries. He laughed about that and declined the privilege.

He preferred to use the regular entrance and go to the same waiting room with the other patients. He introduced himself to each of them, asking their names, even their addresses and phone numbers, so he could keep in touch with them, share their fears and hopes, and pray for them. They became like a new parish for him. As his pancreatic cancer progressed, his bones became brittle. For a man of Italian descent, accustomed to hugging and being hugged, it was difficult to abandon that gesture — even though an embrace could cause a fracture.

By Thanksgiving, it was clear he had little time left to live. He wrote to the justices of the Supreme Court and begged them not to approve physician-assisted suicide. "As one who is dying, I have come to appreciate in a special way the gift of life." He wrote a farewell letter to the American bishops who were gathered for their customary November meeting. He even sent out his Christmas cards early.

A few weeks before he died, he was joined for a prayer service in Holy Name Cathedral by a huge crowd of his priests. His final words to them were touching, warm, and fraternal.

> As our lives and ministries are mingled together through the breaking of the Bread and the blessing of the Cup, I hope that long before my name falls from the Eucharistic Prayer in the silence of death you will know well who I am. You will know because we will work and play together, fast and pray together, mourn and rejoice together, despair and hope together, dispute and be reconciled together. You will know me as a friend, fellow priest, and bishop. You will also know that I love you.
>
> For I am Joseph, your brother.
>
> — JOSEPH CARDINAL BERNARDIN, *THE GIFT OF PEACE*, PP. 141–2

The cardinal's funeral had a festive air, despite the sadness of the occasion. The homily delivered by his close friend and driver, Msgr. Velo, was filled with numerous and humorous stories from Bernardin's life. Msgr. Velo chose an Easter theme based on the Emmaus Gospel: "Didn't he teach us; didn't he show us the way." The homilist used this passage as a celebratory refrain to mark out the sections of his homily — and to great effect.

Cardinal Bernardin never forgot that this life is not the only life. He called death a friend that would transport him to eternal life. "I can say in all sincerity that I am at peace."

Easter in Sacramental Robes

Recently, some have tried to "explain" Easter in rational terms:

- It was an intense religious experience of the apostles.
- It was a clear and lovely memory of the Master.
- It was either a hallucination or a matter of mass hysteria.

The human key to effective preaching of the Word is to be found in the professionalism of the preacher who knows what he wants to say and who is always backed up by serious remote and proximate preparation. This is far removed from the improvisation of the dilettante . . . Care should be taken with the meaning of words, style and diction. Preachers should know their objectives and have a good understanding of the culture of their congregations. Theories and abstract generalizations must always be avoided. Hence every preacher should know his own flock well and use an attractive style that touches their consciences and presents the truth as it really is.

— From *The Priest in the Third Millennium*,
published by the Vatican Congregation of the Clergy

Good evangelical preaching means being able to articulate the religious experience of a community of faith and to call each one to be a disciple and not just a member. . . . The most difficult part of preparing a homily is finding the connection between the Good News and the concerns of the people. A good homily articulates their struggles and illumines them in the light of the Word. What is on their minds? What are their struggles? How do the readings address these concerns? An effective homilist is one who can embrace these concerns and speak from them rather than above them. Nothing is more off putting than the preacher who preaches down to his congregation.

— From a speech by Fr. Thomas Rausch. S.J.,
"Priesthood in the Church of Tomorrow,"
Origins, November 13, 1997

All they have succeeded in doing, however, is explaining Easter away for themselves. I recommend to homilists that they turn to the *Catechism of the Catholic Church* for *sana doctrina*, healthy doctrine about the resurrection of Christ.

I also urge homilists to obtain a copy of *The Resurrection of the Son of God*, by N.T. Wright, the Anglican Bishop of Durham, England. He is one of the best Scripture scholars in the world. His magisterial book on the Resurrection is so full of light, faith, and common sense that his exhaustive masterpiece will become a classic. He begins with the approach of the Greeks to death, the afterlife, and the body. Then, he analyzes the faith of the Jewish people as it grew to appreciate the afterlife and the gift of the resurrection of the body. Lastly, he presents the New Testament teachings on Christ's resurrection, first in Paul and then in each of the Gospels.

Faith and Love

One should approach Easter with a faith enveloped by love. It is the "beloved disciple" John who is quick to sense the reality of the resurrection of Jesus Christ. There is a mysterious link between love and knowledge. Augustine proclaims, "Give me a lover and he will understand." The German poet Goethe insisted, "We learn to know only what we love. The depth and fullness of our knowledge are proportionate to the strength, vigor, and liveliness of our love." Love is blind only to the obstacles of love. Love has the sight of a hawk when seeking truth.

What Does Love See at Easter?

Love sees that Jesus is frequently recognized in prayer events. The Emmaus disciples perceive the risen Jesus in the breaking of the bread. Similar to this is the number of times Jesus appears to the disciples when they gather for shared meals or prayers. He shows himself to those who have gathered together in his name for prayer (cf. Lk. 24:33ff). He discloses himself to the apostles as they gather at the lakeside for a meal. There is a compelling association between the Risen Lord Jesus and the Eucharist. At Capernaum, Jesus had taught that he was the bread of life, and that he would share this gift through the bread that would become his body and the wine that became his blood.

In John's Gospel, we see a strong link between the Easter appearances and the forgiveness of sins — the first intimations of the sacrament of Reconciliation. On Easter night, Jesus appears to the disciples, breathes on them the Holy Spirit of peace, and imparts to them the ministry of reconciliation. "If you forgive men's sins they are forgiven them. If you hold them bound, they are bound."

Something more than a mere physical movement is meant when Mary Magdalene "turns around" to see her risen Lord. Her conversion of heart — her turnaround — is now complete; thus, she is privileged to see the Easter Christ and to be the first one to proclaim his resurrection to the apostles.

The forgiveness theme continues at the lakeside when Peter who had sinned by denying his Lord three times, now makes a triple confession of love and faith. Jesus rewards him with public forgiveness and names him the chief shepherd of the Church. "Feed my lambs. Feed my sheep."

Matthew associates the risen Jesus with the sacrament of Baptism. It is the last scene of Matthew in which Christ is about to ascend into heaven. Jesus commissions the apostles to go forth and preach the Gospel to all nations. They are to teach people to observe all that Christ has commanded. Finally, they are to do this in the context of baptizing people in the name of the Father and of the Son and of the Holy Spirit.

The risen Lord Jesus also uses a Scripture lesson to disclose his resurrected identity. When Jesus explained the Bible to the disciples on the road to Emmaus, they testified that their hearts burned within them with an experience of the divine presence. Through Scripture Jesus prepared their hearts to recognize him in the Breaking of the Bread.

In all these events, love is the key that leads to faith understanding.

What themes do you stress in your Easter homilies?

Risen Lord Jesus, guide me in preaching your resurrection.

People expect more from preachers than they used to.

TWENTY-TWO

Pentecost: Preaching the Holy Spirit

Pope John Paul II (1920–2005): Be not afraid —
overcoming fear of preaching

From the beginning of Christianity, preaching was a major way in which the Gospel became known to the world. "God our Father, you taught the Gospel to the world through the preaching of St. Paul" (*Prayer from the Feast of the Conversion of St. Paul*). Of course, the courageous witness of the apostles and the engaging love of the Christian community and the power of the sacraments were equally contributing factors. But preaching was — and still should be — a powerful and necessary instrument for spreading the faith to others and uplifting the hearts of believers.

The greatest contemporary practitioner of this truth was Pope John Paul II. For over a quarter of a century, this pope traveled to the remotest corners of the world to preach the Gospel, to proclaim Christ. Whether he was in New York's Central Park or a small country church in Iowa, whether he faced a hostile church in Holland or a rapturous crowd in Mexico City, whether he stood humbly before the eternal flame in Jerusalem's Yad Vashem or preached to four million people at World Youth Day in the Philippines, he was always preaching and witnessing the Gospel.

Like St. Paul, he preached in season and out of season, to the rich and the poor, to the secularists and the devout. During his second pastoral visit to the United States, he agreed to a proposal that in each city a speaker would make an address to him about the theme of the day, such as Catholic Education in New Orleans, or Catholic Health Care in Phoenix. His first stop was in Miami, where he went immediately to the Cathedral to meet with priests. Fr. Frank McNulty delivered the address on behalf of the priests. In his remarks, he mentioned the need to reconsider the celibacy rule for priests. To which the pope, with a touch of humor, replied, "It's a long, long road to Tipperary."

While generally the pope stayed with his written text, there were times when he left it and spoke spontaneously — or even sang, as he did during his homily in Central Park, when he was moved to sing a Polish Christmas carol. The emotion of the moment only increased when the Americans responded by singing *Silent Night* to him.

Young people resonated with him even in his last years, when he was so frail and when Parkinson's robbed him of the ability to smile and show feelings in his face. The youth often greeted him with the chant

The Holy Spirit gives us an experience of God, living and active in the Church. The *Catechism* sets out seven ways in which the Spirit provides us with an experience of God's presence. These in themselves are suitable homiletic themes.

1. When we pray and study the Scripture, which the Spirit inspired, we can sense God's presence in the biblical words.

2. When we read the lives of the saints, their teachings, and their witness, we can be motivated to holiness by their example, which was shaped by the Spirit.

3. When we assent with obedience to the teachings of the Magisterium, we are guided by the Spirit. The Spirit's presence is noticeably experienced at Ecumenical Councils.

4. When we actively participate in the liturgies and sacraments of the Church, we enter into a unique situation where the Spirit opens us to experience God, especially in the Eucharist.

5. When we give ourselves to prayer, whether that be the rosary, the liturgy of the hours, meditation, or other prayers, we join the Holy Spirit, who prays with us and intercedes for us.

6. When we offer ourselves to the various apostolates of the Church, we have the charisms of the Holy Spirit providing us with the confidence and energy we need.

7. When we dwell on the Great Tradition of the Church, its marvelous history, and a host of saintly witnesses, we sense the Spirit's sustaining power through it all (cf. *CCC* 68).

"John Paul 2, we love you" to which he replied with a fatherly smile, "John Paul 2 loves you too."

We are all aware of the substantial topics he addressed in his encyclicals. We need to recall that he also preached on those issues such as the Gospel of Life, as opposed to the culture of death in abortion and euthanasia. His Wednesday talks, at the beginning of his papacy, were a unique interpretation of the creation stories in Genesis. Taken together, those sermons have become what is known as the Theology of the Body. John Paul was very interested in marriage and its responsibilities. From his days working with students at the Jagellonian University, he had great sympathy for the challenges of love and marriage they presented him with and sought many ways to counsel the students with his wisdom.

He was a born philosopher, and it showed in his preaching. His studies in phenomenology appeared in his talks and writings. He looked at a given topic from a number of angles. To us it may seem strange; we expect him to move in a logical way, and we wonder why he keeps returning to a thought or image and looking at it in yet another dimension. But that is the method in which he was trained, and it seemed to suit his temperament.

Pope John Paul was a modern St. Paul, preaching Christ all across the world. He had the urge to communicate and was blessed with the voice, the mind, the heart, and the graces — plus the platform that made it possible. The Holy Spirit animated his words and life.

The Holy Spirit and Preaching

The most noticeable aspect of the result of the descent of the Holy Spirit at Pentecost was Peter's sermon. Filled with the Spirit, he stood up and preached a substantial sermon to the pilgrims assembled for the Jewish Pentecost. He filled his talk with references from Scripture and focused these texts on the meaning of the death and resurrection of Jesus Christ. He spoke in such a way that the listeners could not be indifferent to his message. They were "stung to the heart" and asked, "What shall we do?" Peter was prepared and said, "Repent, and be baptized every one of you in the name of Jesus Christ" (cf. Acts 2:38).

Scripture says that three thousand souls were added to the Church that day alone. The Holy Spirit, manifest in the Church through Peter and his preaching, moved a great many people to become Christians.

The rest of the New Testament is filled with the power of preaching and its results: increased membership in the Church and strengthened faith in those who already belong.

Be Not Afraid: How to Overcome Fear of Preaching

1. Face the facts about such fear.
   a. *The Book of Lists* says that fear of speaking in public is one of people's greatest fears; some surveys even place it number one, ahead of fear of death. Forty-one percent of people fear speaking in public, as contrasted to twenty-two percent who fear bugs or financial troubles.

Preaching is more difficult than it was in the days when the priest was the most educated man in the parish and when people were used to listening to and accepting whatever Father said. Add to this that the women and men in our congregations are awash in a sea of words: radios everywhere, faxes and e-mail, beepers and cell phones. There's practically no place to go where you can't be talked at. When today's preacher moves to the ambo on Sunday morning, he probably faces stiffer competition than anybody since St. Paul when he wanted to address the rioting silversmiths of Ephesus. . . . I don't mean to suggest that we are in a golden age of Catholic homiletics but I do believe that priests, deacons and people give more attention to preaching than they used to, and I would expect that this attention will continue to grow as we move toward the parish of the future.

— Archbishop Daniel Pilarczyk,
Speech: "What Will and Won't Change in the Parish
of the Future," *Origins,* Vol. 28, pp. 773ff

b. Some stage fright is useful because it gives you the adrenalin you need to speak with energy. Many professional speakers say they never lose stage fright completely. Even great actors may have it. Laurence Olivier said that the panic of stage fright afflicted him even toward the end of his career. One thing that relaxed him was walking lightly as he entered the stage.

c. The chief cause of fear is lack of experience. To overcome this fear, get as much experience as you can. Teaching helps. In fact, preachers who have been teachers have less fear of giving homilies. The've become accustomed to dealing with students and articulating their topics in a clear and direct manner. I recall a parishioner saying in a complimentary way, "The teaching priest has the nine o'clock Mass this Sunday."

2. Prepare properly.
   a. Only a prepared speaker deserves to be confident.
   b. Know your point. Be convinced about it. Plan your closing.
   c. Perfect love casts out fear. So does "perfect" preparation.

3. Never memorize a talk word for word.
   a. Most people forget what they memorize.
   b. Memorizers think of words. Speakers think of ideas.
   c. Even if you have a good memory, a memorized talk will usually sound mechanical. You are not an actor. You are a homilist.

4. Arrange your ideas beforehand. Brood over your topic until it becomes mellow. Write ideas in a few words and put them on scraps of paper. Place them on your desk and move them around until they "tell" you the sequence.

5. Rehearse your talk with friends. Slip parts of it in your conversation. Tell your opening story to different people at meals or in a walk or during a visit.

6. Lose yourself in your subject. How will you fan the fires of faith in your message? Explore its deeper meanings. Ask yourself, "How will my listeners be better for having heard this?"

What did you do to overcome fear of preaching?

Lord Jesus, give me confidence in my preaching.

The strongest predictor of Catholic behavior and identification is the quality of the Sunday sermon preached in the respondent's parish.

— National Opinion Research Center,
quoted by Archbishop O'Malley, *op. cit.*

TWENTY-THREE

Remote Preparation for Homilies

How God prepared St. Paul to preach: "I am eager to preach the Gospel." (Rom. 1:15)

How Did God Prepare St. Paul to Become a Preacher?

God could hardly have picked a better city in which Paul (Saul) would be born and raised. Alexander the Great conquered it in 334 B.C. and brought Greek culture and education. Then, in 64 B.C., Pompey conquered Tarsus, giving the people Roman citizenship and some degree of self-government.

From the goats grazing on the Taurus Mountains overlooking the city came the raw material that was woven into haircloth to be used to make tents.

Young Saul grew up in this cosmopolitan city, where he received a Greek education, enjoyed Roman citizenship, absorbed democratic ideas, and learned Greek and Latin, in addition to his family language of Hebrew. The higher education of the times stressed rhetoric, which was a combination of public speaking, debate skills, and methods of argument and persuasion.

The final stage in his education took place in Jerusalem, where he studied to become a Pharisee. He was a student of Gamaliel, whose views were sensible, compassionate, and moderate.

God prepared Saul well for the worldwide mission that would be his calling. Bilingual, bicultural, grounded in Scripture and Jewish culture, Paul was ideally suited to be a world-shaking missionary. His training in rhetoric gave him the ability to preach powerfully. His conversion by Christ provided him with the world's greatest message for his preaching.

We all know the , when a blinding light struck him to the ground and he heard a voice saying, "Saul, Saul, why are you persecuting me?" He asked, "Who are you, Lord?" The voice answered, "I am Jesus, whom you persecute. Get up now and go into the city and you will be told what you have to do."

His companions led him — temporarily blind — to the house of Ananias on Straight Street. There, his sight was restored, and he was baptized.

Scripture says that Paul then went to the desert for a long retreat. It was there that God give him an experience the third heaven.

> I will go on to visions and revelations of the Lord. I know a man in Christ who fourteen years ago was caught up into the third heaven . . . caught up into paradise, and heard things that cannot be told, which man may not utter.
>
> — CF. 2 COR. 12:1–6

While Paul was enjoying such ecstasies in the Arabian wilderness, he was rudely jolted by the appearance of a "thorn in the flesh." "And to keep me from being too elated by the abundance of revelations, a thorn was given me in the flesh, a messenger of Satan, to harass me . . ." (cf. 2 Cor. 12:7). God privileged Paul with the ecstasy of paradise to fill him with divine joy — and the thorn in the flesh to fill him with divine humility. These spiritual experiences enabled Paul to preach the Gospel with sublime confidence and a modest heart.

Paul began his missionary preaching in Damascus. Here, he had his first success and his first rejection. So angry did some people become with him that he had to escape in a basket from the city. He journeyed to Jerusalem, where he spent two weeks with Peter. From Peter, he learned vivid details of the life of Jesus. Peter brought him to the spot where the woman was taken in adultery and the house where a woman washed Christ's feet. They walked through the Temple that Jesus cleansed; they walked the Via Dolorosa and knelt at Calvary.

In turn, Paul shared with Peter the story of his conversion, his sojourn in the desert, and his troubles in Damascus. Peter confirmed Paul's mission but felt he needed tempering. Paul's "hour" had not yet come. Peter advised him to return to Tarsus and await the call of the Church. For the next four years, the world's most eloquent preacher accepted the Church's judgment that he maintain a "ministry of silence."

Finally, the Church was opening a mission to Antioch and wanted Paul to help. From then on, nothing could contain the whirlwind that was Paul's passion for the Gospel.

Remote Preparation for Homilies — Our Histories

My sketch about St. Paul dwells on his remote preparation to be a Christian homilist. I began with the question of how God prepared him, then looked at the major formative influences in his life — the tools God used to make an incredible mission preacher. I could have added that Paul was not always a submissive subject to God's will.

God noted his stubborn personality: "It hurts you to kick against the goads" (Acts 26:14). A goad was a sharp prong used to keep cattle in line. Christ was determined to make Paul an apostle and kept goading him until he gave in. Even after his conversion and the spectacular ecstasy God gave him, Paul began complaining about the thorn in the flesh.

> Three times I besought the Lord about this, that it should leave me, but he said to me, "My grace is sufficient for you, for my power is made perfect in weakness."
>
> — 2 COR. 12:8-9

Finally, Paul figured it out and surrendered to God.

> I will all the more gladly boast of my weaknesses, that the power of Christ may rest upon me.
>
> — 2 COR. 12:9

Culture, family background, temperament, education, human weakness, and human strength were the potent mix that God used to make a preacher out of Paul. God does the same for us. God uses our strengths and our weaknesses to be messengers of the Gospel. I believe we come to where we are in the pulpit as a product of lifelong influences, all bubbling beneath the surface, and we hear their subconscious voices behind the words we speak.

We do not escape our history when we open our mouths to feed the multitude. Whether we like it or not, we stand before our congregation

Archbishop Timothy Dolan's practical advice to preachers: The Five S's of a good homily — it is **short, simple, sincere, succinct,** and **substantial.**

1. A good sermon is *short*: KISS — "Keep it short, stupid." This is the major complaint our people have against us — we are too windy. I will get in trouble with some, but anything longer than three minutes on a weekday or ten minutes on a Sunday is counterproductive. Be prepared, be clear, and be seated.

2. A good sermon is *simple*: When I was a deacon, a priest on the faculty said, "Learn to preach well to the fourth-graders. Say it so they can comprehend it well. . . . If you're smart you'll preach that way to everyone." Now be careful! Never do we want to be patronizing or condescending . . . Yet as St. Alphonsus Ligouri wrote, "I must preach so that the most illiterate laborer can understand me." A good sermon is simple.

3. A good sermon is *sincere:* Now this is closely allied to conviction. Our people can quickly detect if we really believe what we are saying. Of course, for a parish priest this means that our sermons have no credibility at all if they do not see us model what we preach in our own life. As the old saying goes, "It is one thing to love to preach; it's another to love those to whom we preach."

4. A good sermon is *succinct*: Fr. Virgilio Elizondo suggested that, in preparing our sermons, we develop "sound bites," colorfully expressing our message in one or two catchy, pithy phrases, since, for better or worse, our listeners are conditioned to receive knowledge that way. The best compliment you can receive as a preacher is, "Father, I wish you had gone on longer." The worst was given by a friend of mine after Mass: "Father, you had a great end to that homily . . . unfortunately, it came about ten minutes before you actually concluded."

5. A good homily is *substantial*: Our people need to hear solid content, doctrinal meat, scriptural lessons, and moral instruction. . . . The temptation today is toward "fluff," cute gimmicks, jargon, trickery, silly stories that take up more time than the message, and excessive use of the "I" pronoun instead of speaking of the Lord. Raw, basic evangelization; primitive, fundamental *kerygma*, solid, faithful catechesis; sound biblical teaching — this is what our people need. You will know you are giving them this when they say to you: "Father, I can always bring something home with me from your sermons." There's a nugget there, something worth saving. A good sermon is substantial.

— Archbishop Timothy Dolan, *Priests for the Third Millennium*, Our Sunday Visitor, Huntington, IN, 2000, pp. 302–305

warts and all, no matter how cleverly we try to hide the deficiencies. The best homilists succeed because they refuse to pretend. They accept their weaknesses and praise God for such gifts. Maybe they are not as forthright as Paul, who boldly boasted of his shortcomings — but, in a lower key, make them a fundamental attitude for their homiletic lives.

Preaching from Strength

At the same time, our strengths float to the surface without any push from our wills. If we are priests and deacons who pray constantly — who are contemplatives in action — that quality will show up in our preaching. All the Gospels describe Jesus taking long periods of time to pray after the exertions of healing and preaching. We fail to imitate him in this regard to our homiletic peril. A prayer-less preacher is a pulpit disaster. We can't hide it. Our people will know it, and their hearts will sink with disappointment. They hope for so much from us, and they pray the preacher will give them bread instead of a stone.

If we are men committed to lifelong learning, both from our life experiences and from a love affair with reading and studying, we will not need to show off in the pulpit. In a quieter and more humble spirit, that quality will penetrate our homilies; they will seem deceptively simple, yet genuinely deep. But the homilist who stops growing mentally, who has lost a child's curiosity about the wonders of life, who has frozen himself at some earlier life stage, will face his people with a dullness in his eyes and a helpless tone in his voice. He can't preach, "I have a dream," because he doesn't.

If we are homilists who love the congregation, who are committed to the daily challenge to love people the way we love ourselves, and love God so passionately that nothing stops us from running toward him, our people will sit up straight with eager faces at our homilies. They need that love made concrete in their shepherds, and praise God when that happens!

In a number of ways, then, the quality of our remote preparation is far more important than the few hours we give to preparing the Sunday homily. It has been said that the unexamined life is not worth living. I think this means that no matter how marvelous or ordinary our life history has been, it always needs self-examination and the resolution to begin again. We need to look again at our autobiographies and see how they make us tick today. What may be stopping us from praying, loving, learning, serving, rejoicing in God, laughing with those who laugh, and weeping with those who cry? When remote preparation is alive and well, then the proximate preparation for homilies will be full of life — and our homilies, in the language of Fr. Robert Barron, will be "words on fire."

What would you consider the remote preparation from your life?

Dear God, thank you for the gifts you have given me.

A prayerless preacher is a pulpit disaster.

TWENTY-FOUR

How to Talk

By Archbishop Fulton J. Sheen —
from his "Life Is Worth Living" TV Series

Probably the most effective preacher of the twentieth century, Archbishop Fulton J. Sheen outlines in this talk many of the principles he followed in composing a speech. We include his talk in this book because a number of his recommendations can be applied to homily preparations and delivery.

Many requests have been received to express some idea on "How to Talk." We will treat this subject on two conditions: first, that we not be considered a model speaker or an orator. It is said that I am an orator, and in weak moments I believe it — but only for the reason that when I finish speaking I notice there is always a "great awakening."

A second condition is that any suggestions that we offer are purely personal. Suggestions will be limited to the way we do it and the way we prepare a discourse. Our method is not necessarily the best. A few years ago I was talking in Canada one Sunday afternoon in a theater. Noticing a collection was being taken as I spoke, I inquired, "What is the purpose of the collection?" The answer was, "To hire a better speaker next year."

The preparation of a discourse. The preparation is both remote and proximate. How long does it take to prepare a speech? How much time is put into a telecast? About thirty or forty years, but this is the remote preparation. It takes only an hour or less to serve dinner to sixty people on an airplane. But the preparation of a dinner actually took months or years. Think of how long it took to grow the carrots, to raise the sheep, to grow potatoes, and to ripen an apple. A good speech, too, has a tremendous remote preparation, and this implies three things: study, study, study. There is no shortcut. Delacroix once said, "Rubens is not simple because he has not worked." There is no simple style, there is only style simplified. One has to study science, literature, history, philosophy, forgoing many social evenings just to be alone with one's books.

Books are the most wonderful friends in the world. When you meet them and pick them up, there are always ready to give you a few ideas. When you put them down, they never get mad; when you take them up again, they seem to enrich you all the more.

Proximate preparation. Here we will spontaneously let a subject come into the mind to show quickly how it may be given immediate development. Suppose we decide to talk about angels, inasmuch as an angel cleans our blackboard.

First we will formulate some general ideas, such as:

1. The knowledge of angels.
2. How one angel affects another angel.
3. The function of angels.

Next we would concentrate on some source material to which we would go to find information on angels. The three best sources would be the Scriptures, Thomas Aquinas and Dionysius. After studying what had been written in these three, we would then fill out our plan.

First, we would show that angels do not know the same way man knows. We derive all our knowledge from below, that is, the sensible world, but an angel derives its knowledge from above. Ideas are poured into an angel's mind by God, as we pour water into a glass.

Next, we would consider how angels affect one another, how the superior angels illumine the inferior angels, like water running down a pyramid. Finally, in treating the function of angels, we would show how some are before the throne of God, how others preside over creation, while others act as special messengers of God.

After a subject is chosen, say, for a telecast, we immediately begin to write out a plan, such as illustrated above, on the subject of angels. We write the general ideas on a sheet of paper; the next day, tear up the paper. The day following we have to start all over doing it again. When that new plan is developed, we tear it up, so that nothing is saved from day to day.

The great advantage of this system is that one is forced to rethink the ideas; the subject is learned from the inside out, instead of from the outside in. Why should the living mind be subject to an inert sheet of paper? A mother does not forget the child of her womb; neither can a mind forget what it has generated by hard thinking.

Today we have only readers on television. There are few speakers any more, and fewer orators. Some believe that what they have written is so sacred that the creative mind ought to bow before a dead message. It is much better, instead of memorizing words, to recreate the ideas each day until the subject is as alive as a child. There may be many mistakes when the time comes to rethink it on your feet, but at least there is this consolation, it is *your* talk. Whenever we hear anyone read a talk, there is always the temptation to ask, "Who wrote it?"

Much wisdom is hidden in the remark of the old Irishwoman who heard a Bishop reading his discourse. She said, "Glory be to God, if he can't remember it, how does he expect us to?"

Three conditions of a good talk are sincerity, clarity, flexibility.

Sincerity. To have sincerity is to be without affectation, pose, or cultivated airs; just being oneself. The word "sincere" has an interesting origin. When the Romans found pieces of marble that were imperfect, they put wax in the holes. Wax in Latin is *cera.* When they found a perfect piece of marble, it was called *sine cera,* or without wax, whence comes the word "sincere." A sincere speaker is one without guile or artfulness. If the tongue gives forth an uncertain sound, who will prepare for battle?

One of the first rules in speaking is: Do not imitate Bishop Sheen. No imitator is sincere. Be yourself! Every person is unique and incommunicable. There is something about him that is worth more than the material universe. Having his own tempo, his own spirit, his own disposition, he ought to speak out of that, and he will be interesting.

Insincerity often is derived from a want of conviction or truthfulness. So many people say things they do not mean that when they really want to drive home a conviction they lack the power to move. How different is the tone of the voice of an announcer when he reads his commercial from when he describes a baseball game. He does not believe in the commercial, so he lacks sincerity. Lincoln once said that he liked to hear a man talk as if he were fighting bees. Too often men dedicated to religion pray in public either as if they were giving marching orders to God or as if they were more interested in the audience than in God. In some instances, it would be better to tell the audience to pray rather than to pray *to them.*

A lesson in sincerity was given me in college. I was chosen for the debating team, and on the night before the Notre Dame debate, our professor of debating called me to his office and scolded me.

"You are absolutely rotten," he declared. "We have never had any-body in the history of this college who was a worse speaker than you."

"Well," I said, trying to justify myself, "if I am so rotten, why did you pick me for the team?"

"Because," he answered, "you can think; not because you can talk. Get over in that corner. Take a paragraph of your speech and go through it."

[I did so, over and over] again for an hour. At the end of that hour, he said, "Do you see any mistake in that?"

"No."

[So I did it again, for] an hour and a half . . . two hours . . . and finally, at the end of two and a half hours, I was exhausted.

"Do you still not see what is wrong?" he demanded.

Being naturally quick, after two hours and a half [sic], I had caught on. I said, "Yes, I am not sincere. I am not myself. I do not talk as if I meant it."

He left me with the final injunction, "Now you are ready to speak."

As Shakespeare expressed it:

To thine own self be true,
And it must follow as the night the day,
Thou canst not then be false to any man.

Clarity. Clarity is derived from understanding a subject. A professor in a class in cosmology once asked me the definition of time. I said, "I know what it is, but I can't tell you." He said, "If you knew what it is, you could tell me."

The reason why professors are dull in class is that they do not understand their subject. The ordinary teacher of physics could not tell an uneducated person about the mathematics of space-time. But Eddington and Jeans have done so, because they knew the subject profoundly. It is easy to write a book with footnotes, because everything you do not understand or do not grasp thoroughly you put down at the bottom of the page, so that someone else can look it up. But to write on that same subject so that children in the seventh or eighth grade can understand it, one must really understand the subject.

The ideal talk possesses clarity for both the educated and the simple when it combines abstract principles or scientific description with concrete examples or analogies. The educated can follow both: the uneducated can grasp the idea at least vaguely through illustrations drawn from their own experiences. Our Blessed Lord, who is the eternal Word, did not disdain to use parables to make mysteries clearer to our finite minds. One must always know more about a subject than one gives in a speech. As the lungs must have the atmosphere, as the eye must have more light than that which enters it, so the mind to breathe easily on a subject, must have a great environment of knowledge.

Clarity is aided by telling the audience what you are going to do. Give them the points of the discourse. Then they know at least when you are going to finish. Otherwise, if one appears with a sheaf of papers, the audience after an hour may sigh, "He has two more inches to go." At a philosophical convention, a speaker was reading a paper on "Essence and Existence" for an hour and a half. The listeners were exhausted until he looked up from his page and said, "I forgot to tell you I have three carbon copies here of my speech." It was such a relief!

In television, one must always time himself from the end, not the beginning. Decide how many minutes one needs for the conclusion. Suppose it is three minutes. Then just three minutes before the appointed time, swinging gracefully from the body of the talk to the conclusion, one finishes "right on the nose."

Flexibility. Readers should always be ready to skip over about eighty-nine pages if they see the audience tiring. Then, too, there maybe interruptions; someone faints, or someone may be heckled. A speaker was once addressing a group of lawyers. One lawyer was in a state of "amiable incandescence." He stood up, shouting something which nobody understood. As everyone turned to him, the speaker said, "You have been practicing at the wrong bar."

I recall a drunk once standing up in the gallery, heckling in a most unintelligible manner. After failing to catch his words, I seemed to satisfy him with the observation, "The only man who likes to be interrupted in the middle of a sentence is a prisoner."

Once, when I was giving instructions to a convert class in Washington on the Blessed Trinity, someone began to heckle me about Jonas: "How was Jonas in the belly of the whale for three days?" I said, "My good man, I do not know. But," I said, "when I get to heaven, I will ask Jonas." He said, "Suppose Jonas is not there?" I said, "Then you ask him."

On another occasion when I was preaching in a small country parish, a mother, embarrassed by her crying infant, left the pew to leave the church. "I said, Madam, it is quite all right. The child isn't bothering me." She said, "I know, but you are bothering the child."

Flexibility is increased when one does not have the speech memorized; then one can make use of any occasion that may arise in the course of the discourse. Recall the beautiful impromptu speeches of our Blessed Lord, such as the one to the woman at the well, when he turned the subject of thirst into the idea of the soul's yearning for God.

More important than the above factors in preparing a discourse is to recognize that every speaker is a trustee of God's truth. When we speak, we are only the flute; it is God who breathes on us. We supply only the quality of tone — nothing else.

Prayer and meditation are essentials for a truthful message. The last thing I do before giving a talk is to go into the chapel, kneel down before Our Lord in the Blessed Sacrament, and say to Him, "Give me strength, tonight, to speak thy Truth, that Thou mayest be known. not me; the power to make others love Thee, so there may not be only truth communicated but also a love of that truth."

Light and heat are inseparable in fire, and they ought to be inseparable in anyone who gives a discourse. The light is God's truth; the heat is the tremendous love with which one ought to communicate the truth. To love what we say, it must be true. To want to speak the truth, it must be loved.

— Fulton J. Sheen, *Life Is Worth Living*.
Ignatius Press, San Francisco, 1999, pp. 191–197

Homily Resources

The *Catechism of the Catholic Church*. Check this to help your homily have a sound doctrinal basis.

The Priest Magazine. Sunday Homilies in each issue (Huntington, IN: Our Sunday Visitor).

Magnificat. PO Box 91, Spencerville, MD 20868-9978 (helpful for both Sunday and daily homilies).

Footprints on the Mountain, Preaching and Teaching the Sunday Readings, ABC., Roland Faley, T.O.R. Mahwah, NJ: Paulist, 1994 (each commentary is followed by suggested homily topics).

Illustration Digest, Quarterly Publication of stories, PO Box 170, Winslow, AR, 72959 (Lots of good stories. Also check the many versions of *Chicken Soup for the Soul* at your Barnes and Noble or Amazon.).

Fr. Joseph Champlin's books on Marriage and Funerals: *Through Death to Life* and *Together for Life* (check Amazon.com).

Books of Homilies by Walter Burghardt, S.J.(check Amazon.com).

Parochial and Plain Sermons by Cardinal Newman. San Francisco, CA: Ignatius Press, 1987.

Three-minute sermon resources

I especially recommend *Word on Fire* by Fr. Robert Barron (hear him on radio or via streaming audio on the Internet).

Also . . .

My Daily Visitor, Our Sunday Visitor.

Internet Resources: Google the word "homilies."

Woodeene Koenig-Bricker, *365 Saints: Your Daily Guide to the Wisdom and Wonder of Their Lives.* New York, NY: HarperSanFrancisco, 1995.

Mark Link, SJ. *Vision Year A; Mission Year B; Action Year C*. Allen, TX: Thomas More, 1992, 1994, 1998.

Enzo Lodi, *Saints in the Roman Calendar*. Staten Island, NY: Alba House Publishers, 1992.

Some Scripture Resources

Since homilies are principally explanations of Scripture as it applies to the faith and life needs of the listeners, useful biblical resources are helpful and often necessary. Remember that the Scripture readings are from divine revelation/God's Word, calling us to **faith** in the divine plan of our salvation. Every homily should be evangelizing.

1. The Jerome Biblical Commentaries, both old and new.
2. The Interpreters Bible Commentaries, both old and new.
3. The Anchor Bible Commentaries, especially Raymond Brown's on John's Gospel and Joseph Fitzmeyer's commentary on Luke.
4. *Harper Dictionary of the Bible*.
5. William Barclay's *Commentaries on the New Testament* (oldie but goodie!) provides a lot of colorful background about Scripture. Makes homiletic applications. Although short on Catholic teachings such as the Eucharist, Mary, Saints, Church, and Popes, it's still very readable.
6. Navarre Scripture commentaries — Scripture at top of page and comments from Church Fathers at bottom.
7. Commentaries and Meditations on Matthew, Mark, Luke, John, Acts, and Revelation, by Alfred McBride (Our Sunday Visitor). Easy access material, does not cover every story or passage.
8. On the Internet may be found commentaries from the Fathers of the Church, translated by Oxford Scholars in the nineteenth century, titled *Ancient Christian Commentaries on Scripture*. Heavy going.
9. Carroll Stuhlmueller, *Biblical Meditations for Ordinary Time*, weeks 10–22.
10. *The Acts of the Apostles* (Sacra Pagina Series) by Luke Timothy Johnson and Daniel J. Harrington.

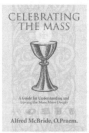

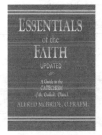

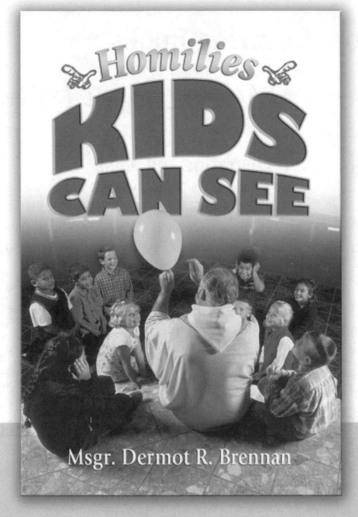